TRADITIONAL SEASONAL
COUNTRY COOKING

TRADITIONAL SEASONAL COUNTRY COOKING

90 timeless farmhouse recipes using fresh, natural ingredients

Beautifully illustrated with over 400 step-by-step photographs

SARAH BANBERY

southwater

This edition is published by Southwater
an imprint of Anness Publishing Ltd
Blaby Road, Wigston
Leicestershire LE18 4SE

Email: info@anness.com
Web: www.southwaterbooks.com;
www.annesspublishing.com

If you like the images in this book and would
like to investigate using them for publishing,
promotions or advertising, please visit our website
www.practicalpictures.com for more information.

Publisher: Joanna Lorenz
Senior Editor: Felicity Forster
Designer: Design Principals
Jacket Design: Nigel Partridge
Recipes: Pepita Aris, Catherine Atkinson, Alex Barker, Ghillie Başan,
    Georgina Campbell, Carla Capalbo, Miguel de Castro e Silva,
    Lesley Chamberlain, Carole Clements, Matthew Drennan,
    Jenni Fleetwood, Brian Glover, Christine Ingram, Bridget Jones,
    Lucy Knox, Janet Laurence, Sally Mansfield, Maggie Mayhew,
    Anna Mosesson, Keith Richmond, Rena Salaman, Jennie Shapter,
    Christopher Trotter, Suzanne Vandyck, Laura Washburn,
    Biddy White Lennon, Carol Wilson, Annette Yates
Photographers: Nicki Dowey, Ian Garlick, Amanda Heywood,
    Janine Hosegood, Dave Jordan, William Lingwood, Steve Moss,
    Craig Robertson
Production Controller: Christine Ni

ETHICAL TRADING POLICY

© Anness Publishing Ltd 2011

Previously published as part of a larger volume,
The Illustrated Practical Book of Country Cooking

NOTES

Bracketed terms are intended for American readers. For all recipes,
quantities are given in both metric and imperial measures and,
where appropriate, in standard cups and spoons. Follow one set of
measures, but not a mixture, because they are not interchangeable.
Standard spoon and cup measures are level.
1 tsp = 5ml, 1 tbsp = 15ml, 1 cup = 250ml/8fl oz.
Australian standard tablespoons are 20ml. Australian readers
should use 3 tsp in place of 1 tbsp for measuring small quantities.
American pints are 16fl oz/2 cups. American readers should
use 20fl oz/2.5 cups in place of 1 pint when measuring liquids.

Electric oven temperatures in this book are for conventional ovens.
When using a fan oven, the temperature will probably need to be
reduced by about 10–20°C/20–40°F. Since ovens vary, you should
check with your manufacturer's instruction book for guidance.

The nutritional analysis given for each recipe is calculated per portion
(i.e. serving or item), unless otherwise stated. If the recipe gives a
range, such as Serves 4–6, then the nutritional analysis will be for
the smaller portion size, i.e. 6 servings. Measurements for sodium
do not include salt added to taste.

Medium (US large) eggs are used unless otherwise stated.

Although the advice and information in this book are believed to
be accurate and true at the time of going to press, neither the
authors nor the publisher can accept any legal responsibility or
liability for any errors or omissions that may be made nor for any
inaccuracies nor for any harm or injury that comes about from
following instructions or advice in this book.

Main front cover image shows Roast Pheasant with
Sherry Mustard Sauce – for recipe, see page 80.

CONTENTS

Introduction

Country cooking is essentially based on traditional peasant food that has evolved over the centuries. The authentic recipes of the countryside naturally rely on good ingredients and fresh seasonal produce, making use of all the fantastic richness of locally produced food throughout the year. Peasant and country dishes also include many more esoteric foods such as oysters and game which are today regarded as luxury items, but in the past would actually have been classified as poor man's food.

The hard-won knowledge and frugal habits of the country cook, developed with patience and skill over time, are reflected in our 21st-century concerns with the origin and provenance of ingredients. We are beginning to understand that local, fresh, seasonal produce has a better flavour and is far more nutritionally rich than food that is imported from far-flung countries out of season, and this is an area where country recipes shine.

The age-old custom of passing down tried-and-tested traditional family recipes from generation to generation, along with cherished cooking skills, equipment and utensils, means that country food has survived to be appreciated and enjoyed by each new generation of cooks.

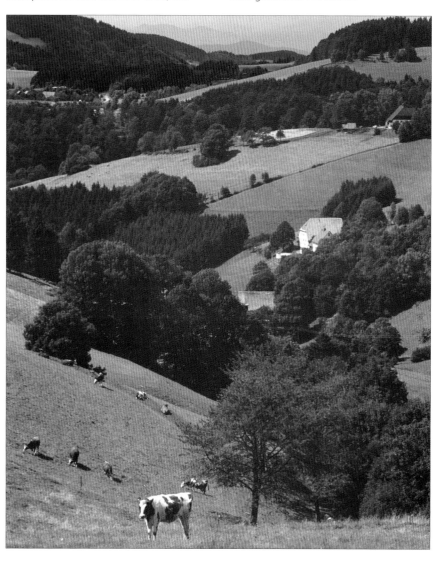

The contemporary country kitchen

With a growing interest in cooking seasonally, in using organic produce and the simplest, freshest ingredients, the contemporary country kitchen retains much of what is best about traditional cooking, but with the added blessing of modern equipment, time-saving gadgets and appliances. Innovations such as pressure cookers and bread machines mean that the busy home cook can now recreate many of the more time-consuming recipes of the past in a fraction of the time, without losing any authentic taste. In modern kitchens, it is easier than ever to make the most of all the fresh, high-quality ingredients on which country cooking is based.

Home-made food

Country cooking is simply delicious home-made food using traditional raw materials, without any unnecessary waste. For example, many meat dishes involve long, slow cooking, making use of every possible part of an animal such as the trotters, the head and the offal. This thrifty custom has played a key role in developing some of the best-loved country meat recipes.

An integral part of this style of cooking was preserving food, which was an absolute necessity rather than an indulgence. Home baking and home smoking, along with pickling and salting, and making cheese and butter, were a natural part of living in the country and a matter of pride. Many a country larder contained neat rows of preserved fruit and vegetables in jars, with maybe a ham or some game hanging on a hook and a crock of salted fish ready to be eaten in the cold

Left Summer in the country means rich grazing for farm animals and an abundance of produce from the woods, fields and vegetable plot months of winter. Techniques such as making a rich stock from meat bones or vibrant crab apple jelly from windfall fruits illustrate the inventiveness that characterizes much country cooking.

The seasons

Culinary creativity was very important to the country cook, whose life revolved around the seasons. Traditional recipes tended to be structured around one central ingredient which was in season – spring vegetables tasting wonderful in a delicious soup, or pork as the main ingredient of a raised pie, for example. If there was an abundance of one crop, it was either used fresh in different ways or stored for the cold weather.

Spring could still be a time of year when the cook was largely reliant on preserved foods to support the few early vegetables, while the summer months provided plenty of fresh fruits, vegetables and salads from an overflowing kitchen garden. In the autumn, the country cook has traditionally relied heavily on wild foods to support the larder and pantry. Game from the fields and woods, as well as hedgerow fruits and nuts, complemented the last of the

summer crops. Winter recipes reflect the thriftiness of country cooking, with hearty stews making the most of the root vegetables, brassicas and dried beans and peas, and using bottled and pickled vegetables from the store cupboard to bulk up meagre winter crops.

Country traditions

The simple act of baking a certain loaf of bread or a special cake for a specific celebration or festival evolved over time to become an indelible part of country tradition. These rituals, treasured and passed down within families, connected people both to the rhythms of the countryside and to the traditions of their local community, marking the passing of the year. Harvest suppers, spiced Christmas drinks, festival sweetmeats and Easter cakes are all concocted from ancient recipes in the country kitchen.

Today, spending time in the kitchen baking a fruit cake, chopping home-grown vegetables to make soup or cooking wonderfully nutritious food

Left Country cooking techniques often rely on a few well-loved utensils, such as this traditional rolling pin, pastry cutters, mixing bowl and jug.

Above Savoury roast joints of meat and sweet pies are delicious when cooked with home-grown local fruits, such as these beautiful apples.

from a few simple ingredients reconnects us to the countryside. Even growing a few herbs in pots on the window sill or making your own preserves can give a satisfying feeling of keeping up time-honoured culinary customs.

About the book

This book begins with a description of country cooking, its history and methods, including some fascinating facts about the practical cooking techniques of our rural ancestors.

The second chapter gives an overview of the typical ingredients used in country cooking, from orchard fruits and wild foods to fish, poultry, meat, dairy produce, eggs and flour.

Next, there are eight chapters of recipes, ranging from simple, rustic soups and pot roasts to some best-loved regional specialities, puddings, breads and preserves. Many dishes can be prepared ahead of time or slow-cooked all day in traditional fashion, bringing the real taste of the country to your table.

Country traditions

Throughout the centuries, cooks have prepared food for the family using whatever ingredients were available. Peasant cooking relied entirely on goods from the local area, fresh and in season, plus whatever could be preserved by bottling, pickling, salting or drying to eat when the kitchen garden was covered with snow and the wheat fields were bare. Today we can be inspired by the thrifty methods of the past to make delicious meals that everyone will enjoy.

The history of country cooking

The development of our traditional cooking has its roots in pre-history. The earliest cooking would probably have been limited to roasting meat and game on a spit, toasting and grinding grain and using simple hollowed-out stones and bones to heat liquids over an open fire.

Early cooking techniques

Not until the development of settled agriculture and the introduction of pottery would cooking develop beyond the most basic methods. By the Middle Ages the resourceful country cook, restricted by the limitations of one-pot cooking on an open fire, relied on tasty dishes such as soups, stews and casseroles, spit-roasted meat and preserved fruit and vegetables for many months of the year. Bread dough was baked in a central public oven, since most of the rural populace would not have access to an oven at home.

Tools, equipment and utensils

From mankind's earliest days, much effort was put into developing tools for gathering, killing and cooking food. Clay, iron and bronze materials were

Above Cherished kitchen utensils and equipment were often passed from one generation of cooks down to the next.

fashioned into pots used for cooking over the fire and also for preserving food. Utensils made of wood and metal, such as ladles and knives, became stronger and more reliable.

Well-tested techniques for preserving food were vital. As well as preserving fruit and vegetables in glass jars or earthenware crocks, many rural homes would smoke fish and meat in the chimney or in a home-built smokery.

The cook now had access to a broader range of cooking equipment, as well as specialist dairy tools for making butter and cheese. The Victorian era saw the introduction of a huge number of new cooking utensils and mass-produced kitchen gadgets such as fancy pastry cutters, cheese graters and potato peelers.

Fires and ovens

Cooking food over an open fire is the basis upon which all subsequent cooking has developed. The earliest pot ovens, domed iron pots placed over hot hearth stones, gave way to clay or brick-lined ovens similar to today's

Left Fruits such as cranberries, together with spices and herbs, were important ingredients for preserves.

pizza ovens, but until the end of the 18th century, much cooking was still done over an open fire. Iron stoves began to appear in the late 18th century, but it was not until the 'cooking machines' or closed stoves appeared in Victorian kitchens that home cooking was really revolutionized.

By the 19th century the typical farmhouse kitchen had a fireplace with a chimney and a rudimentary range with its own ovens. The Aga stove or range cooker and other coal- or wood-fired ovens used today are still associated with a more traditional cooking style; they have certain limitations, but these stoves are often much loved by their owners, who have become experts in slow-cooking skills.

Larders and pantries

Keeping food fresh was a constant concern for the country cook. Storing vegetables and fruits in a cool place on stone floors with a good circulation of air meant they lasted longer. Eventually a larder cupboard or walk-in pantry was

Left The American plantation kitchen had an open hearth for cooking, a hand-cranked meat mincer and copper pots.

exchange an excess of produce. These markets became the focus of many rural communities, with people travelling long distances, often on foot, to buy and sell the essentials of life. Many towns and settlements grew up around the site of a regular market, and in some countries the right to hold a market was a highly valued privilege enshrined in writing. Although both regular markets and seasonal fairs were essentially trading institutions, they became a treasured part of the life of the country. In recent eras, when many countries have seen an increase in trade and movements of population, markets played an integral role both in the dissemination of new foods and cooking styles and in the preservation of ancient local customs.

constructed in every rural kitchen, as well as in many town basement kitchens. This was the ideal place to keep dairy products and meat in the best condition before the advent of refrigeration. It was also a good place for keeping dry stores of beans, peas and grains, and preserved foods and vegetables in glass or earthenware jars. Many farmhouses in dairy farming areas developed their own clean, cool dairies where the scrubbed stone floors and shelves gave the best conditions for making and storing butter and cheese.

Local markets

Markets were integral to country life and the rural economy. They developed from the basic need to barter or

Below Fruit, vegetables and preserves are kept cool and dry in a pantry, along with dried herbs and garlic.

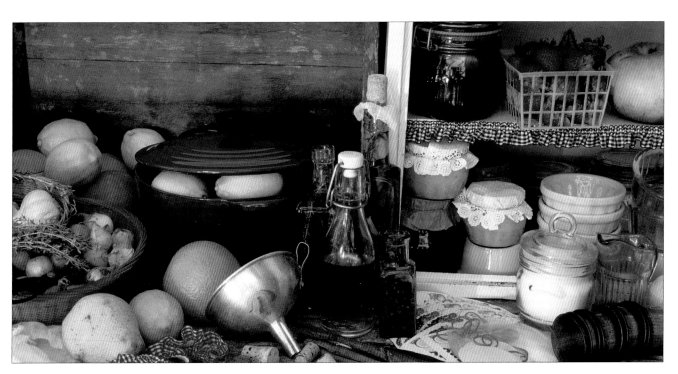

Frugal food

For the earliest farmers, the earth needed to be coaxed into fertility, and their hard-won skills gradually developed over many years as a response to the challenges of living off the land. The popular image of the countryside as a bucolic and tranquil place belies the reality for rural communities all over the world; the poverty and hardship of country living has always demanded an inventive and frugal way of life. Almost all country cooking relies on good sense, forward planning, a talent for improvisation when times are hard and shared skills rooted in long experience.

Making the most of the countryside

Country economy is symbolized in the use of absolutely all parts of an animal. One or two pigs were often kept in country yards to be killed and eaten in the winter – an essential source of protein for the peasant farmer and his family. Virtually no part of the pig was thrown away: once the major cuts had been eaten as roasted joints and the lesser ones as stews, fat was rendered for lard, intestines were used for sausage cases, and hearts were stuffed and braised. In many countries of the world, pig's feet and ears are a delicacy.

Recipes using ingredients collected from the wild also bear witness to the country cook's frugal outlook. These delicious dishes include soups made from wild greens, herbs and even nettles. Game, fish, nuts and seeds were all hunted or collected to enrich and diversify the country diet. Foraging for food was considered not just a source of free ingredients, but also a positive pleasure when the day could be spent hunting or fishing, picking blackberries along a field edge or searching for mushrooms in the woods.

Economical food around the world

Around the world, peasant cuisines show a great regard for frugal economy. Since peasant food traditionally uses whatever ingredients the local land has to offer, it is always both accessible and inexpensive, and often based around a limited number of staple, hearty ingredients cooked in a single pot.

Left To make the most of a pig, the meat was salted, smoked or preserved, and also made into sausages.
Right Home-grown tomatoes are perfect for cooking if you can resist eating them as soon as they are picked.

Above Good economy means taking advantage of what the fields, woods and hedgerows have to offer.

Scarcity of ingredients has led to great culinary invention in many countries, with the creation of new dishes and exciting ways to present familiar ingredients. In Turkey, for example, there are countless recipes based on the simple aubergine (eggplant), examples of which can be found in glistening deep purple piles in every market. These include the famous aubergine and tomato dish, Imam Bayildi.

In many countries, traditional meals vary only slightly across the borders, where the climate and ingredients are similar. The peasant dishes of Germany, such as Himmel und Erde, puréed potato and apple with blood sausage, and Sauerbrauten, a sweet and sour pot roast served with dumplings and cabbage, both remain distinctively German but share a common culinary heritage with other 'peasant' foods such as Irish Stew or French Cassoulet. The technique of marinating and slow cooking the less tender cuts of meat such as the shoulder, shanks and ribs resulted in mouth-watering casseroles, pot roasts and stews.

Waste not, want not

Leftovers feature prominently in country cooking. In Italy, rice left over from a risotto would be added to soups or made into Arancini – balls of cooked rice stuffed with cheese and deep-fried. Spanish Gazpacho, Italian Pappa al Pomodoro and English Queen of Puddings were all made to use up stale bread. Pizza is the ultimate peasant dish, a flour and olive oil dough base topped with tomato sauce and whichever vegetables and cheese are available.

Sourcing ingredients today

With the rise of the grass-roots movement that promotes traditionally raised food, today's resourceful cook can take advantage of the best their country has to offer. Financial imperatives paired with an increased desire to buy good, natural food means that many people are more educated about where their food comes from and what they should pay for it. Awareness of the amount of pesticides used in commercially grown crops and the less welcome effects of agro-chemicals and antibiotics used to rear livestock intensively means that many people are beginning to buy

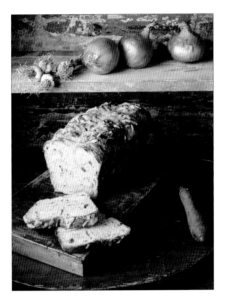

organic and bio-dynamic foods instead. In particular, the furore over the advent of genetically modified crops has starkly illustrated the number of artificial processes associated with modern food production. In contrast, vegetable and fruit varieties grown organically may take longer to grow and have lower yields of uneven-sized crops, but they have time to develop more flavour and are nutritionally richer.

The reintroduction of traditional and rare-breed animals and an increased concern for animal welfare means that

Left A thick slice of home-baked bread, such as this cheese and onion loaf, is a delicious and filling country snack.

many more livestock and poultry are raised free-range and slaughtered in more humane conditions. Meat can often be sourced from farmers as many rural producers now sell direct to the consumer. Buying a whole or half animal from a farmer, butchered into convenient portions and ready for the freezer, means fantastic meat at a reasonable price.

Growing your own is the best way of ensuring freshness, but there are also increased opportunities for sourcing frugal ingredients. Farmers' markets, farm shops, co-operatives and box schemes offer locally grown and organic supplies which are, by definition, in season and fresh. Buying food from the person who grew or raised it has the added benefit of the exchange of knowledge, ideas and perhaps even recipes. In this way, the city-dwelling cook with an interest in traditional food can bridge the gap between urban and rural life.

Below Free-range meat from animals such as these sheep can be sourced direct from farmers and markets.

The kitchen garden

Growing fruits, vegetables and herbs has always been an integral part of the self-sufficiency of the country cook. A well-planned kitchen garden will provide an ongoing supply of fruit and vegetables throughout the year – just as one crop is coming to an end, a new one will take over – and as long as the cook has enough skill and imagination to make the most of a glut, to preserve everything that cannot be eaten immediately, and to plan ahead so that best use is made of the available space, the kitchen garden can be an inspiring place.

The renewed interest in 'growing your own' means that planting a kitchen garden is no longer solely the privilege of the rural population. Allotments, land shares, community gardens and urban plots, or even a pot or two in a small yard or on a windowsill, make home-grown fruits and vegetables available to all.

Nowadays, there are plenty of dwarf varieties available that crop well but take up limited space. Even vegetables such as runner (green) beans or aubergines (eggplants) – which would usually need a large area to grow in – can now be grown in containers on patios.

Grow your own

One of the major advantages of home-grown food is that it encourages the country cook to make recipes that are prepared from scratch. Having a handy selection of your favourite fruits, vegetables and herbs flourishing just outside the kitchen window is a huge help – and also an attractive addition to any back garden.

In order to avoid making expensive mistakes, it is a good idea to check the gardening catalogues for ideas and maybe borrow some books from the library before you start. There is plenty of practical advice to be had on the best varieties to grow, whatever the size and shape of your plot. The traditional varieties of many vegetables, including 'heirloom' varieties, often

Left Damsons are ideal for jam-making, and the trees look very pretty in spring with their snow-white blossom.

Above This neat kitchen garden has a recently harvested crop of onions drying on the ground before being stored.

taste fantastic, and you will have the additional pleasure of knowing that you are preserving our culinary heritage.

Containers and window boxes are a great way to start growing vegetables because they are manageable and can be very productive. Some climbing varieties of fruit and vegetables do not need deep soil and can be grown in grow bags or containers in a small space. A small herb garden or pots of herbs on a windowsill will offer an easy introduction to growing at home, with the attraction of fresh ingredients to hand for cooking. There is nothing quite like the aroma of a dish of new potatoes with home-grown mint or parsley sprinkled on top.

Another big incentive to start cultivating a small plot or vegetable garden is that it is an easy way to

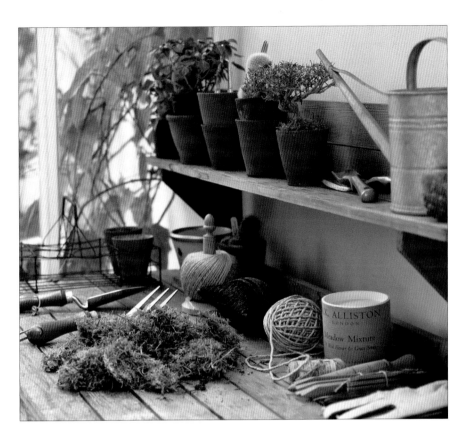

While many crops can be harvested gradually over a long growing season, other fruits and vegetables will have a short but extravagantly abundant burst of activity, providing a big yield in just a few weeks.

For this reason, preserving has long been an integral part of getting the most from a home harvest, helping to avoid groans from the family as they face yet another courgette (zucchini) or tomato dish for supper. While many crops will freeze well, some fruits and vegetables do not respond favourably to this treatment, becoming soggy or tasteless, and so the old traditional methods of making jams, jellies, relishes and chutneys, and bottling, drying, salting and pickling come into their own.

The great value of home-made preserves is in capturing the colours, textures, smells and tastes of summer at any time of the year. There is also the undeniably warm glow that comes from eating your own produce, preserved in your own kitchen, all year round.

Above *A space for potting seeds is useful when growing fruits and vegetables at home or in an allotment.*

introduce children to new fruits and vegetables which they might otherwise be reluctant to try. Windowsill gardening is ideal for children, as they can inspect the crop regularly.

Vegetable gardens can also be much more than a working part of the garden. Certain fruits and vegetables, such as potatoes, onions, lettuce and the dwarf varieties of beans, can be integrated into an ornamental garden, although this is not an easy option – both vegetables and flowers are going to need constant attention to keep them pest-free and avoid one variety swamping the others. Even if there is no room in the flower garden for vegetables, many fruit trees flourish against a sunny wall and also look extremely decorative, with their spring blossom and autumn fruits.

Plot to pantry

Growing fruit and vegetables can very easily result in over-production of certain varieties at particular times of the year.

Below *Home-grown thyme, asparagus, onions, figs, radishes and carrots can go straight from the garden to the kitchen.*

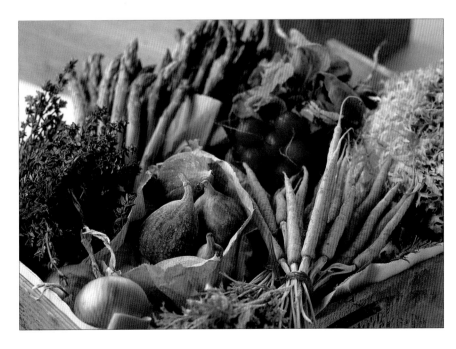

Seasonal food

Eating seasonally is as relevant today as it was centuries ago. Cooking and eating within the year's natural rhythm means that fruit and vegetable varieties are eaten when they are at their best in terms of flavour and ripeness, as well as nutritional qualities.

But it is not only the taste and goodness of traditional fresh food that should focus everyone's minds on buying seasonal produce. An increasing concern about the impact of fossil fuels used to transport foods from far-flung countries has added to the renewed interest in cooking and eating local produce. Awareness of food miles and reluctance to pay a premium price for tasteless out-of-season foods are now coupled with a desire to support local economies and reconnect with the seasons.

Seasonal recipes

In many regions of the world, shopping every day naturally means having the choice of produce restricted seasonally – but often this is no hardship as long as the cook is prepared to settle into a pattern of traditional cooking dictated by the harvests. This is where growing your own or buying local fresh produce

Above *Spring carrots are best when lightly cooked and simply served with butter and some chopped parsley.*

really pays dividends. Newly harvested fruits and vegetables that are cooked on the same day they are picked retain their natural goodness and will be eaten before their natural sugars turn to starch, thus making them sweeter and more flavoursome; they often have a better texture and cook more quickly.

Everyone can tell the difference between a bowl of fragrant, firm strawberries eaten at the height of the harvesting season in early summer, and the tired, soggy, tasteless examples bought in midwinter. But this also applies to other ingredients such as tomatoes, courgettes (zucchini), new potatoes, peaches, spring lamb and many more. Why not make good use of all these wonderful flavours when they are at their absolute peak?

Left *Succulent summer fruits such as strawberries are delicious in fruit fools, with ice cream or in a sweet pudding.*
Right *Orchard apples are perfect for autumn puddings such as crumbles, or baked with dried fruits and honey.*

Spring

As the first spring produce appears, it is time to move on from the casseroles and stews of the winter months and enjoy the vibrant new flavours of spring vegetables and early fruits. The best way to cook these fantastically fresh ingredients changes from long, slow cooking to quick stir-fries and grilling (broiling), or even serving raw in a salad.

Early spring is the ideal time to use up the last of the winter staple crops and pair them with new herbs and dressings, perhaps using the first wild greens in a casserole or simmering the new pink shoots of rhubarb and blending them with cream to make a tasty dessert. Later, spring shoots and tender young vegetables such as broad (fava) beans and new potatoes make interesting salads, and this is also the time of year when luxuries such as asparagus start to appear.

Summer

The sunshine brings the opportunity to make plain but exquisite dishes focusing on the best-quality ingredients. Early summer offers young, sweet vegetables

Left Many fruits and vegetables are at their best in the autumn, such as these pumpkins and squashes.

Winter

The colder months may be restricted in the variety of seasonal foods available, but winter is the time to bring out the preserved and stored foods hoarded in the summer and preserved in the autumn. There are still some fresh vegetables available, such as cabbages and Brussels sprouts, which do not reach their peak of flavour until the first frosts.

Late autumn cooking apples and berries can be stewed or baked in a pie. Beans and peas are a good store cupboard stand-by at this time of year and can be made into warming dinners for winter evenings; they taste great paired with root vegetables. Steamed puddings are essential winter warmers, and a home-baked fruit cake bursting with dried fruits is a tempting treat for the winter store cupboard.

Below Winter is the season for root vegetables, citrus fruits and dried fruit, which can be stored until needed.

such as new potatoes, lettuce, peas and beans; later, the focus moves to sun-ripened tomatoes and bell peppers, courgettes, marrows and main-crop potatoes. The soft fruits in the kitchen garden – raspberries, strawberries, peaches and apricots – are perfect for desserts such as fruit fools and tarts.

Cooking with warm weather in mind means making simple, light food – delicious fresh dishes such as chilled soups, salads, grilled (broiled) meat and fish, for example – to allow the flavour and texture of the produce to shine. Summer is also a good time to turn a glut of soft fruit and summer berries into cordials and cooling drinks, which are very welcome on a hot day.

Autumn

As summer draws to a close, the thrifty country cook begins to preserve the abundant harvest of fruits and vegetables and to make jams, pickles and other preserves. The autumn season is blessed with an overlap between the last of the summer produce and the first of the root vegetables and brassicas,

with the opportunity to start making hearty soups and roasting pumpkins, squashes, potatoes and parsnips.

Autumn is also the season for game, wild mushrooms and nuts, as well as being the perfect time to start making treats for Christmas such as fruit cake, pudding and presents of bottled fruit or spicy chutney.

Preserving and storing

Smoking, drying, bottling or making jams and chutneys are all major activities in the country kitchen. These techniques are really worth learning, even in an era when all kinds of foodstuffs are available the whole year round in the supermarket. Eating your own preserves, made with best-quality, tasty fruits and vegetables, is a reminder of summer in the depths of winter. There is no comparison between a cheap shop-bought strawberry jam with its high sugar content and red colouring, for example, and the darker colour and richer, purer flavour of home-made strawberry jam, bursting with fruit.

Jams, jellies and marmalades

Making delicious jams and jellies is the most common way to enjoy the summer's harvest all year round. Jams and jellies are particularly versatile preserves, with many uses in the country kitchen – they can be spread between the layers of a sponge cake, used as a dessert topping, or simply served with freshly made bread for tea.

Jam is made by simmering prepared fruits, either whole or chopped, with sugar. Fruits that are low in pectin, such as strawberries, make a soft-set jam, whereas those that are naturally full of pectin, such as plums or gooseberries, make a firmer preserve. Compôtes are simply soft-set jams made with a little less sugar, served fresh, as they will not keep for long. Many traditional jellies are made from hedgerow crops such as crab apple, mint and elderflower, and these delicately flavoured preserves are usually served with meats or cheese.

Old-fashioned fruit butters and cheeses are preserves made with the fruit pulp left in a jelly bag after the juice has dripped. Making fruit butter requires less sugar than jam and the texture is softer – perfect for spreading.

Fruit cheeses have a firmer texture and are made from well-sieved (strained) thick fruit purées, often from fruits with lots of pips or stones such as damsons or quince. In contrast, fruit curds are made with the addition of butter and eggs, gently cooking the fruit to create a thick, sweet conserve which has a shorter shelf-life than other preserves because of the dairy content. Piquant lemon curd is the best known, but other fruits such as gooseberries, apricots and quince also lend themselves well to this treatment.

Marmalade is made in a similar way to jam, using citrus fruits. The fruit rind in marmalade needs longer cooking than the usual jam fruits, so water is

Above Home-made jams and jellies look very attractive when finished with pretty tops, to give as gifts.

added to the fruit and sugar while it is cooked. The marmalade can be flavoured with alcohol or fragrant spices such as ginger.

Pickles, chutneys and relishes

Both fruits and vegetables can be made into mouth-watering pickles and chutneys. Chutney is made with chopped fruit and/or vegetables simmered with varying amounts of spices, sugar and vinegar to a thick pulp and then stored in jars. As it improves with age, chutney stores very well and has a long shelf-life. It is particularly useful for using up end-of-season fruits such as windfall apples and green tomatoes, mixed with dried vine fruits such as sultanas (golden raisins) and currants.

In contrast, pickles are more often made with whole vegetables, such

Far left Stone fruits such as these ripe plums can be bottled, or made into jam, chutney or a rich fruit cheese.
Left Some autumn fruits, if carefully wrapped and properly stored, can last for many weeks or months into winter.

Far left *Fruit or herb jellies are often served with roast meat, but are also delicious with cold pies or cheese.* **Left** *Many herbs can be air-dried by tying them into bunches and hanging them in a cool, dry place.*

as baby onions, cauliflower florets or beetroot (beet). The vegetables are first salted or soaked to remove excess moisture, then packed into jars and covered in vinegar, with the addition of strong herbs and spices to add a really zingy taste to the mixture. Pickles do not require the long cooking of chutney, and benefit from being kept for a few weeks for the flavours to develop.

Both pickles and chutneys are usually served straight from the jar with cold meats, terrines, pies or cheese, but they can also be regarded as an instant ingredient to add zest to many winter dishes. Pickled onions can be rinsed and added to a robust casserole or stew, for example.

Relish is halfway between chutneys and pickles. It consists of coarsely chopped fruit or vegetables, spices and vinegar cooked together for a shorter time than chutney, so the vegetables tend to keep their shape. There are even traditional recipes for uncooked relishes that make the best of a summer glut – vegetables or fruits such as tomatoes, courgettes (zucchini), bell peppers or plums can be chopped and mixed

Right *Pretty bottles can be re-used for pickling if they are sterilized and have new, air-tight tops.*

with chillies, herbs and seasoning and served cold. These should be kept in the refrigerator and used within a few days.

Bottling

The technique of bottling is most often used for preserving best-quality whole fruits and vegetables. Fruit is usually bottled in syrup or alcohol to keep the colour and flavour of these pristine ingredients; vegetables are more often bottled in brine. Fruit and vegetables for

bottling must be fresh and not too ripe. Stone (pit) fruits such as apricots and plums are particularly suitable for this method and look glorious with their beautiful colours shining through the glass jar.

Drying

Home-drying fruit and vegetables was long regarded as an important part of preserving. Dried vegetables are oven-, sun- or air-dried, and then often packed in oil, while dried fruits are kept in boxes. Fruit, vegetables and herbs will keep for many months when properly dried, and most characteristically have a particular intensity of flavour. Sun-drying crops such as tomatoes, aubergines (eggplants) and bell peppers is popular in the Mediterranean, India and the Middle East, where these vegetables grow easily and the sun is strong enough to preserve all the goodness quickly.

The country kitchen

Country recipes rely on traditional cooking techniques
combined with the quality and freshness of good produce.
Focusing on natural, seasonal ingredients will enable any
cook to produce wholesome food which is both healthy and
delicious. This chapter gives an overview of all the basic
ingredients used in country cooking, from the familiar fruits
and vegetables of the kitchen garden to autumn berries and
nuts, and from meat and dairy products to fish and shellfish.

Garden, field and orchard

In the past, most country gardens contained a few vegetables, a fruit tree or two and maybe a beehive or some chickens – all with one aim in mind, to put food on the table. Nowadays, many rural and city gardeners are turning at least part of their flower beds over to food production, and expressing an interest in traditional methods of harvesting, cooking and preserving. Even city-dwellers with no garden usually have access to the most wonderful fresh, seasonal produce in their local shops and markets.

Vegetables

The vegetable garden was always the basis of country cooking. Gardeners knew how to prepare the ground, rotate their crops to get the best from the nutrients in the soil and raise as many excellent vegetables as they could cram into their plot.

Bulb vegetables, including onions and shallots, garlic, leeks and salad onions, have always been a favourite in the country kitchen. They provide a quick and easy way of adding depth of flavour to many dishes.

Leafy greens and brassicas include broccoli, Brussels sprouts, cauliflower, cabbage, spinach, endive and salad leaves – all of which are best eaten very soon after picking.

Root vegetables such as potatoes, carrots, squash and parsnips are amazingly versatile winter vegetables. Often used as thickening agents in casseroles or stews, they can also be mashed, roasted, puréed or made into delicious velvety soups.

Peas, broad (fava) beans, French (green) beans, borlotti beans and corn grow prolifically but need lots of space, and should be harvested while young.

Asparagus is slow to establish in the garden and has a very short season, but should not be missed. Other summer vegetables that need the full warmth of the sun to ripen include tomatoes, bell peppers, avocados and aubergines (eggplants) – these grow well in hot countries or under glass in cooler areas.

Dried beans, peas and lentils

The number of varieties of the dried seeds of plant legumes runs into thousands. As they are inexpensive,

Above Courgettes are part of the squash family, which also includes pumpkins, marrows and gourds.

easy to grow and have a good storage life, dried beans, peas and lentils have long been an integral part of the country diet. They are high in protein and complex carbohydrates, low in fat and nutritionally rich.

Bean stews, salads, soups and casseroles, re-interpreted for each culture, appear in recipes from all over the world, such as Tuscan Ribollito or Southern Succotash Chicken Soup from the United States. Beans, peas and lentils can also be puréed and mashed into delicious dips and pâtés or included in curries and highly spiced meat dishes.

Fruits

An enormous number of fruit varieties are now available. Among the best-known are tree fruits such as apples, pears and quinces, which appear in the late summer and autumn, while stone (pit) fruits such as apricots, cherries,

Left A variety of healthy vegetables and fruits has always been part of the rural diet, especially in the summer.

Left Peaches and apricots are fragrant summer fruits – they are perfect in a sweet dessert or for making jam.

damsons, greengages, nectarines, peaches and plums tend to ripen earlier in the year.

Soft fruits and berries include bilberries, blackberries, black, white and red currants, blueberries, gooseberries, raspberries and strawberries, and are mainly summer and autumn crops, some of which can be found growing wild in the countryside.

Grapefruit, oranges, lemons, limes, mandarins and kumquats need consistent warmth and sunlight to flourish; in northern parts of the world they can only be grown indoors. Bananas, dates, figs, mangoes, pomegranates, melons

and pineapples are some of the best-known 'exotic' fruits that can only be grown in hot, humid climates or in a heated greenhouse.

Central to the country larder is a good supply of preserved fruits, which keep well and can therefore be imported from warmer countries to the cooler parts of the world: dried vine fruits such as currants and sultanas (golden raisins) appear in numerous traditional European cakes and biscuits, and dried dates, figs and apricots are used extensively in Mediterranean and Middle Eastern savoury dishes.

Nuts

In country cooking, nut butters are often used to thicken soups and stews or added to stuffings and sauces, and nut oils are made into fragrant dressings. French cooks use walnuts and chestnuts extensively, and in Italy almonds are a staple ingredient, with

Left Each variety of nut has its own distinctive taste. Nuts can either be added to dishes or eaten as a snack.
Right Fresh herbs add essential flavour to country meals, and are very easy to grow on a sunny windowsill.

fragrant almond paste central to many seasonal celebration dishes and sweetmeats. Sweet chestnuts are also made into chestnut flour, which used to be a substitute for the more expensive wheat flour in peasant kitchens.

Seeds

Pumpkin seeds are delicious roasted and tossed with a little sea salt and eaten as a snack. Pine nuts, sesame seeds and sunflower seeds are all important, nutritionally rich elements in peasant cooking throughout Europe, North Africa and the Middle East, and form the basis of many traditional dishes.

Herbs

Easy to grow and versatile, herbs can be used fresh or dried, cooked or raw in both savoury and sweet dishes, and each has its own distinct flavour and texture. In slow-cooked recipes, a bouquet garni added at the beginning of cooking allows the flavour to permeate throughout the dish, while a sprinkling of chopped parsley or coriander (cilantro) on a bowl of cooked rice or vegetables adds freshness and colour.

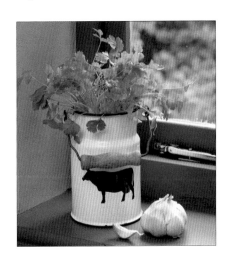

Wild foods

In the past, foraging for wild roots and fruits was a vital part of country life, providing nutritious, succulent treats to supplement the kitchen garden and store cupboard. Wild food can also add variety and indeed a luxurious, unexpected flavour to some traditional dishes.

Rural cooks have always regarded the hedgerow and field as an extension to their larder, and this tradition survives today, with many families enjoying a day out with a picnic to pick the produce of the countryside. As long as care is taken to avoid poisonous varieties of fungi or polluted bushes near main roads, wild mushrooms and hedgerow fruits such as blackberries, elderberries and rosehips still present great possibilities for making delicious meals. They can occasionally be found in magnificent abundance, and the opportunity for preserving a glut of berries in the form of jam or jelly, for example, should not be missed.

Depending on your location, there is usually some sort of wild food available for gathering in every month of the year, including nuts and berries, wild greens, roots, herbs, seeds and flowers such as elderflowers and rosehips. In the early spring, there is a 'hungry gap', when the last winter vegetables are finishing, the spring vegetables have not yet appeared, and the store

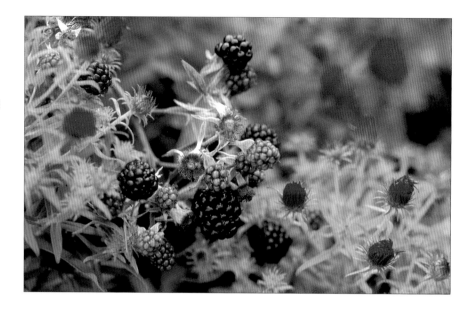

cupboard is emptying fast. At such times, wild food such as watercress, nettles and mushrooms have been essential additions to the country diet.

Fruits and berries

In Europe, the autumn and early winter is a particularly rich time for foraging, with fruits such as blackberries, damsons, juniper berries, sloes, crab apples and rosehips all ready for picking.

The tradition of pickling, bottling and preserving these fruits and vegetables, storing nuts and drying fungi are all methods by which the country cook bolsters the store cupboard. In Spain, wild quince is customarily made into Membrillo, a sweet quince paste. Fruit wines, syrups and drinks made from windfall fruits feature in many cultures: cider made from apples, elderflower or damson wine and rosehip syrup are all traditional treats. Fiercely alcoholic vodka, gin and other spirits, made from

Left These tiny, bright red crab apples can be harvested in the autumn to make tasty home-made apple jelly.
Right Full of healthy vitamin C, rosehips can be used for making delicious teas, syrups and jellies.

Above Hedgerows are a great source of wild berries, such as these blackberries which make lovely bramble jam.

bland grains or root vegetables, are often flavoured with herbs and berries such as juniper or sloes that were gathered in the autumn.

Green leaves

Since most cultivated vegetables are descended from native ancestors, there are many greens and leaves growing wild which make good additions to the cooking pot – spinach, nettles, rocket (arugula) and sorrel all grow abundantly and are delicious. Italian family recipes for Minestrone soup often include wild greens, such as dandelion leaves. English cooks often use horseradish root and mint made into piquant sauces to accompany a roast joint of meat.

Mushrooms and fungi

Wild mushrooms grow throughout the year, but autumn is often the most rewarding time for harvesting fungi because this season offers such an abundant and varied selection. They are delicious, but there are some varieties that are extremely poisonous. It is essential to take a good guidebook with you to identify edible varieties, or find an expert to check your collection. Bear in mind that many highly poisonous varieties look remarkably similar to edible ones.

Like many uncultivated foods, wild mushrooms tend to have a superior flavour to cultivated varieties, and they also have their own distinct texture and taste. Some fungi are found in large abundant groups, while others are less easy to spot. Many wild mushrooms dry very well, and highly prized varieties such as morels and ceps are an important winter ingredient in Italy and Spain.

Unlike most other foraging, mushroom collecting requires focus, knowledge and commitment, and especially so if it is truffles that are being hunted. In France and Italy, these are the most highly prized fungi, requiring great skill and commitment to find – preferably with the help of a truffle hound or pig to sniff out these delicacies.

Herbs and edible flowers

When collected from the wild, herbs generally have a stronger flavour than commercially cultivated varieties. They may grow in great profusion, and

armfuls of some herbs can be gathered and dried for use in winter cooking. Native herbs tend to have an affinity with local foods. Hardy, woody-stemmed herbs such as rosemary, thyme and oregano grow prolifically in hot climates, and their pungent aroma works best when cooked with strong-tasting meat and fish, but they can also be used for infusing oils for cooking. More delicate herbs such as basil, sorrel or chervil are better used raw with vegetable, fish or chicken dishes.

Edible flowers such as nasturtiums and dandelions have been used for centuries, not just for their visual appeal but also for their delicate flavour in salads or preserves.

Folklore often credits these foods with beneficial properties – many herbs, flowers and wild foods are still used as remedies, such as feverfew for headaches and peppermint to aid digestion.

Fish and shellfish

Saltwater fish, freshwater fish and shellfish have long been recognized as a vital source of protein and minerals, supplementing the country diet of vegetables, cereals, dairy and meat. The earliest hunter-gatherers foraged the coastline for shellfish, and tidal zones of the seashore provided valuable sea vegetables, including seaweed.

Fish

There are countless classic fish recipes, and shellfish such as crab and prawns (shrimp) also appear in local dishes all over the world. Freshwater crayfish and eels, long considered peasant food, have been re-invented for the modern cook, and appear on menus alongside more glamorous companions such as scallops and oysters.

As many of our oceans are now over-fished, dishes once made to use up unwanted leftover fish from the catch – such as Bouillabaisse from southern France – are now regarded as rather a luxury. Smaller fish such as sardines, mackerel and herring, once the staple diet of Portuguese, Spanish and northern European fishermen,

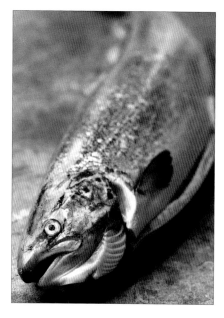

are replacing fish such as cod, whose stocks are diminished through pollution and over-fishing.

Drying, salting, pickling and smoking were all traditional methods of preserving before canning and freezing procedures became available, and many countries have their own techniques depending on the variety of fish – for instance, tasty pickled or soused herring from Scandinavia, strong-flavoured smoked

Above left Large whole fish such as sea bream or this sea bass are perfect for poaching or oven-roasting in foil. *Above* Wild salmon is delicious poached and served warm or cold with home-made herb mayonnaise.

mackerel and salmon from Scotland and the acquired taste of salt cod from Spain and Portugal.

The seasons affect fish, just as they do the fruit and vegetable crop. It is worth investigating when native varieties are at their best, in terms of abundance and availability. Seasonality as the foundation of traditional cooking means that locally caught fish will give a really authentic flavour and texture.

When buying fresh fish, look out for unclouded, bright eyes, firm flesh and pink gills, and a pleasantly fresh aroma of the sea rather than a strong 'fishy' smell. Delicate white fish responds best to simple baking, steaming or grilling (broiling), perhaps with a few herbs and butter, while more substantial, meatier fish can take bolder handling and richer sauces.

Left Fast-flowing inland rivers and streams are good sources of freshwater fish such as salmon and trout.

Each country has its own native species and plenty of traditional dishes to match; it is worth experimenting with whatever fish is available locally, as many recipes are transferable, but you should keep to the right kind of fish – white fish, flat fish or the nutritionally rich oily fish species.

Shellfish

The term 'shellfish' covers crustaceans such as prawns and shrimp, langoustines, lobster and crab, as well as molluscs and cephalopods such as clams, oysters, scallops, mussels, cockles, winkles, cuttlefish and squid.

Traditionally harvested from the sea shallows and caught in inland waters, shellfish proved a useful part of the diet of early mankind. Oyster and clam shells have been found in the archaeological remains of many of the earliest peoples, from the Aborigines of Australia to the Celts of the Scottish Outer Hebrides. Most shellfish recipes make the most of the delicate, salty flavour of these tasty morsels by cooking them when they are really fresh; some, such as oysters, are generally eaten raw.

Cured and preserved fish

Fish has been preserved in many different ways since ancient times. Drying, smoking, salting or preserving in vinegar or oil was once essential if the fish was to be enjoyed out of season. Freezing and canning have largely supplanted older methods of preservation, but smoking is still popular – less for its preservative qualities than for the texture and flavour it imparts.

In the pre-refrigeration days, salting fish was a necessity to preserve it on the long sea journey from the fishing grounds to port, but nowadays the salting process is more commonly used to create luxuries such as smoked salmon. The salting process draws moisture out of the fish, and as it dries, the flesh firms up, making it easier to carve and changing both its flavour and its texture.

Salt cod, or bacalao, as it is known in Spain, is still very popular in many European countries, and is used in dishes such as Brandade and Salt Cod

Right Coastal communities have the advantage of choosing from the catch of the day as it lands on the quayside.

Fritters. Salted and preserved anchovies were traded as long ago as Roman times, and salted, cured fish roe – Bottarga – remains a favourite food of the Portuguese.

Smoking preserves fish by a hot or cold smoking process. In cold smoking, the fish is first cured and then smoked at low temperatures for anything between 24 hours and 3 weeks. In contrast, hot smoking effectively 'cooks' the fish, as it is smoked at a higher temperature for between 6 and 12 hours.

Smoke houses have evolved slightly differently around the world, but generally the principle is the same: fish are salted, rinsed and then strung up to air dry, and finally smoked over smouldering woodchips or peat. The strength of the cure and length of smoking affects the colour and flavour of the fish, and adding sugar, juniper berries or other flavouring to the flesh will change its character. Oily fish such as eel respond particularly well to smoking.

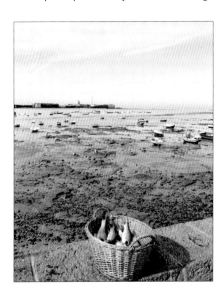

Poultry and feathered game

Many a country garden, from the most prosperous farm to the tiniest cottage, once had a group of hens happily pecking in the dirt, jealously guarded by the resident cockerel, or a few ducks swimming on a tiny pond. These creatures were a fantastic source of eggs and meat and would be carefully protected from marauding foxes. Out in the woods and pastures, country people also had access to feathered game such as partridge, pheasant and grouse, which would be hunted and then cooked to make a tasty autumn or winter casserole, with their rich, dark flesh.

Chicken

The most popular and widely available poultry, chicken is a staple in most kitchens around the world, even though these days they are often bought in markets or shops. Traditional recipes use the whole bird; once the flesh of the chicken has been eaten, there is still the liver to make into pâté and the carcass to boil with a few vegetables for a rich jellied stock.

As with all country cooking, recipes have developed over the years to make the most of the kind of chicken available, whether it is a young spring chicken, at its best simply roasted with fresh herbs, or a laying hen past its

productive years, which is ideal for casseroles with plenty of vegetables and a full-flavoured gravy.

Traditional country chickens would have been raised in conditions now defined as 'free range' – they would have lived mainly in the open, foraging and feeding outside, eating a varied diet of grains and scraps from the kitchen, with plenty of space to establish their pecking order. The free-range and organic chickens now available in many shops and markets are likely to have a similar flavour and texture to those found in the traditional farmyard.

Above Organic free-range chickens are reared in the open air with plenty of space and opportunities to forage.

Turkey

Once only appearing at Thanksgiving or Christmas, the large, domesticated descendant of the North American wild turkey is now available all year round, as a whole bird, leg pieces or breast pieces. It makes a splendid roast dinner for a special occasion, accompanied by lots of vegetables and a light stuffing packed with fresh herbs.

Guinea fowl

Until recently regarded as game birds, guinea fowl are slightly smaller than chickens and have a more pronounced, stronger flavour; the hen birds are considered to be more tender. Sold as squabs, chicks or fowl, they can weigh

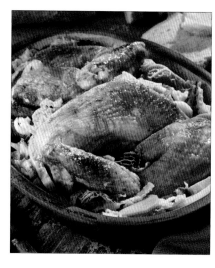

Far left A traditional roast turkey with all the trimmings is central to Christmas and Thanksgiving celebrations.
Left Guinea fowl are perfect for a casserole or a pot roast slow-cooked with fresh seasonal vegetables.

up to 2kg/4½lb, and are cooked in similar ways to chicken – they can be either roasted whole or sliced into pieces to make a delicious dish with a creamy sauce.

Duck and goose

These were traditionally wild game birds, but both duck and goose are now more widely available as they are bred and raised commercially. The rich flesh of duck and goose blends particularly well with orchard fruits such as apples, pears and quince, whose tartness cuts through the strong flavour of the meat. In France goose is often eaten with prunes. Goose was the proud centrepiece of many traditional English feasts and celebration meals, especially at Christmas.

Feathered game

Wild birds hunted for the table have long been a staple country food, being readily available in the woods and fields of many rural areas, mostly during the autumn and winter months. Wild birds tend to have a stronger flavour and denser texture than domestic poultry. Young game birds are usually roasted, and older birds are braised or stewed in much the same way as domestic chicken.

While the countryman would shoot his own, birds such as pheasant and quail are now reared commercially, and are widely available in shops and markets. Rarer birds such as grouse and woodcock are usually found only at specialist game dealers.

Perhaps the most widely available game bird is the pheasant, which originated in China and is related to the chicken. They are usually sold as a 'brace' – a hen and a cock bird – and the two birds are cooked together, roasted or braised in a large casserole dish with vegetables, herbs and spices such as juniper berries. As with most game birds, pheasant are low in fat and lean, with a strong, distinctive flavour, which develops according to how long they have been hung.

Grouse are truly wild game birds. They include the sage and red grouse, and the capercaillie, particularly prized for its distinctive flavour and lean flesh. The smaller birds are highly prized for their rich flavour; a single bird such as

Left Goose has a rich, fatty meat that is delicious when served with berry sauces or fruit jellies.
Right The classic way to prepare partridge is to roast it whole with strips of bacon, and serve with cabbage.

Above left *A male or 'cock' pheasant, with its colourful head feathers, is a common sight in the autumn woods.*
Above *Grouse are a wild game bird hunted only for a limited season, and much prized for their flavour.*

partridge, pigeon or quail will serve only one person. Quail are pink-fleshed and succulent, quick to cook and often available part-boned. Their attractive speckled eggs are often used in canapés.

The rarest and most prized wild birds are woodcock and snipe. Both have dark, intensely flavoured meat, and are usually roasted whole (including their intestines and head) and served one per person.

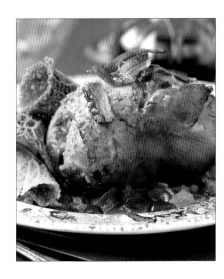

Meat and furred game

Central to the country diet, both domestically raised meat and wild game have always been a prime source of protein. While there are plenty of traditional recipes for roast meat as the centrepiece of a special meal, many country recipes call for the cheaper cuts of meat or offal, which work so well in rich, tasty stews and casseroles cooked gently and slowly in the oven.

Beef, lamb, pork and offal

The meat from domestic cattle is one of the most prized sources of protein, used in both everyday and celebration meals around the world. Generally 'prime' or 'rare' beef comes from a pedigree herd, while 'dairy cross' comes from a dairy cow, and veal is the paler, tender meat of a young calf up to the age of six months. Traditional methods of cooking beef vary hugely, depending on the cut, including everything from a standing rib roast of the best, most succulent meat to a homely shepherd's pie made of beef mince (ground meat).

Good-quality lamb should have light red, moist flesh with a good layer of firm, creamy fat. The leg and shoulder are usually roasted, but again there are plenty of lesser cuts that melt into tenderness when simmered slowly in stock with some vegetables and mint from the garden. In past centuries,

mutton was preferred to lamb because of its richer flavour; it has been unfashionable and difficult to obtain but is undergoing something of a comeback with the revival of interest in our culinary heritage.

Domesticated pork was regarded traditionally as a seasonal meat, much of which was processed, preserved and salted to provide ham, bacon and sausages throughout the winter. Good pork should be pale pink with creamy white fat and a pliable rind.

As 'rare breed' pork is now becoming fashionable again, many excellent and diverse traditional breeds have made a comeback.

Above There are many different kinds of beef cattle. Hand-fed animals will produce the most tender meat.

Offal was a natural part of the diet in the days when nothing was wasted from a precious carcass. It can be really delicious, and there are many traditional recipes from around the world for sausages, fricassees and casseroles made with these strong-tasting ingredients. Pig's blood is also used to make black pudding, known as Boudin Noir in France and blood sausage in Germany and the USA.

Preserved and processed meats

Age-old techniques of preserving meat include curing methods such as salting, pickling, air- or wind-drying and smoking. One of the best meats for preserving is pork, which makes delicious joints such as ham and bacon. These were once the mainstay of a farmhouse pantry.

Far left Young prime lamb chops are best simply cooked quickly on a griddle, barbecue or grill, with rosemary.
Left A stuffed tenderloin of pork wrapped in bacon to keep the meat moist makes an impressive lunch dish.

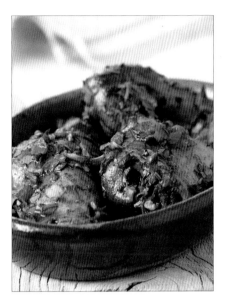

Far left *Good sausages have a high meat content. Pan-fry them and serve with pickles and home-made bread.* **Left** *Young rabbit and hare can be roasted, but are also good slowly casseroled with wine and vegetables.*

(ground) meat. Venison is often marinated in red wine with tart juniper berries to tenderize the meat, and has a great affinity with other astringent fruits such as blackberries and redcurrants.

The smaller furred game such as rabbit and hare, which populate the countryside, naturally feature in many country recipes, and lend themselves to a wide variety of cooking methods, from casseroles to pies. Hare is larger and less common than rabbit, and is considered a delicacy, with its moist, rich flesh and distinctive flavour.

Wild boar meat is more widely available in recent years. Traditionally a game animal, this sturdy wild pig is hunted across Europe and prized for its rich, dark meat. It makes a wonderful stew with a full-bodied flavour.

Below *Sheep which have grazed on particular ground, such as salt marshes, provide meat with a distinctive flavour.*

Pâtés and terrines are a good way of using up leftover meat. The difference between the two is that a terrine usually contains layers of meat that are immediately visible once the dish is sliced up, whereas a pâté is a smoother, more blended mixture. Cold raised pies are simply a variation on the terrine, where pastry replaces the dish in which terrines are cooked. Traditional raised pies with lard-rich, hot-water pastry can last up to a month, and make perfect picnic fare.

Sausages are another important staple of country cooking, whether they are fresh, smoked or dried. Fresh sausages are made by blending chopped meat – usually pork – with fat, seasonings and spices, fresh or dried herbs, cereal or rusk stuffed into cleaned intestines. Sausages can be made from virtually any blend of meat, game or poultry, and some varieties contain no meat at all – the French country sausage andouillette, for instance, is made from tripe.

Dried sausages, such as salamis and chorizo, have been air-dried to extend the amount of time they will keep and, like North African merguez sausage, might have chilli and other dried herbs or spices added to them.

Furred game

Game animals, like game birds, are a vital part of the country kitchen. These days, venison is more likely to come from farmed deer than to be caught wild. The meat is dark and lean, and can be cooked in similar ways to beef, with the saddle, haunch and loin best suited to roasting and the fillet or boned loin providing a juicy, well-flavoured steak. Lesser cuts of venison can be slow-cooked or made into sausages or minced

Dairy produce and eggs

The country cook has always had access to the freshest milk, cream and eggs, and dairy produce is a very important part of rural cooking. Before the advent of the centralized dairy, many homes had their own cow for providing milk and a few chickens for fresh eggs. Making butter, cream and cheese was a regular ritual and a delicate skill often handed down among the women of the family. Any excess produce was useful for trading, and always found a market.

Milk, cream and yogurt

Domesticated cows, sheep and goats provide milk for the country kitchen, and this can be processed into wonderful thick cream and sour cream, butter, yogurt and cheeses of all kinds and flavours. Buffalo and camels also produce milk, providing a staple food for many cultures.

A rich source of calcium and vitamins, and infinitely versatile, milk can vary in fat content, with the richest full-fat (whole) milk being the best type for cooking.

Traditionally, buttermilk was the liquid left over after churning milk into butter, but today it is more likely to be formed by the addition of lactic acid bacteria to milk, creating a liquid with a thickish texture between milk and yogurt. With its piquant flavour,

buttermilk is used for pancakes, scones and bread, and for tenderizing meat or poultry before cooking.

Double (heavy) cream has a high butterfat content, and is therefore the most frequently used cream for cooking. Whipping cream and single or light cream have much less butterfat and are not so suitable for cooking, but they add richness to a sweet pudding or a white sauce.

Crème fraîche and sour cream are both manufactured products that can add creaminess and bite to a dish. Before the introduction of pasteurization, crème fraîche was created when the bacteria naturally present in cream fermented and thickened. Sour cream

Above Old-fashioned dairy containers like these were often made from pottery to keep the contents cool.

was made by letting fresh cream sour naturally, the acids and bacteria occurring in the cream producing a thick textured cream with a slightly acidic taste, ideal for stirring into savoury soups and casseroles or for adding a twist to a rich, sweet dessert.

Below left Dairy cows provide milk for a range of products, including butter, cream, yogurt and cheese. *Below* Enamel bowls were used for separating curds from whey, and enamel pint pots for measuring milk.

Above Dairy butter, made into blocks or 'pats', was used fresh or salted down to preserve it for longer.

Above This farmhouse goat's cheese has a thick rind, showing it has been aged and has a well-developed flavour.

Yogurt is the bacterial fermentation of milk, to create curds. The most common is made from cow's milk, but sheep and goat's milk also makes good yogurt with a more tangy taste. Probably originating from India, Asia and southern Europe, yogurt may well have been introduced to the rest of the world by travelling nomads. As it has been made for thousands of years, there are many regional varieties. Greek (US strained plain) yogurt is strained to reduce the water content and produce a richer, thicker variety that can easily stand in for cream as a dessert topping. Middle Eastern yogurt – labneh – is thicker still, and used in many savoury dishes.

Butter and cheese

New butter was an everyday luxury in the country for those with access to fresh cream. It was churned from cream and then formed into butter 'pats' or 'rolls', and wrapped in linen or vine leaves to keep it cool and clean. Butter was used fresh and unsalted in the spring and summer, with any surplus salted down to help preserve it for autumn and winter. It is essential in

many cake and biscuit (cookie) recipes, lending flavour to a plain sponge cake or light pastry. It is also used in savoury sauces, or mixed with herbs and seasoning to melt over a simple fish dish or a grilled (broiled) steak. In India, ghee is made by heating butter and straining out the impurities, and this clarified butter is used widely in traditional country cooking.

Cheese, the most versatile and portable of all milk products, can be made from almost any type of milk. Some cheeses are produced with a mixture of two or three types of milk,

such as Greek halloumi and feta. The final flavour and texture of the cheese depends on many factors: the type of milk used, what other ingredients are added and how long the cheese is aged or matured.

Eggs

Fresh eggs are an integral part of country cooking, and are a hugely versatile ingredient. Hen's eggs are the most readily available, but duck, goose and quail eggs are also useful additions to the country kitchen – there are numerous traditional recipes which make the most of them in omelettes, cakes and savoury tarts.

Eggs should be kept cool in a pantry or refrigerator, but always brought up to room temperature before use. Always choose the freshest eggs available, especially for recipes such as mayonnaise or chocolate mousse, which use uncooked eggs. Vulnerable groups such as babies and the elderly should avoid eating raw egg.

Below left Free-range and organic chickens lay eggs that have a bright yolk colour and are nutritionally rich. *Below* The freshest eggs should always be used for recipes that are made with raw egg, such as mayonnaise.

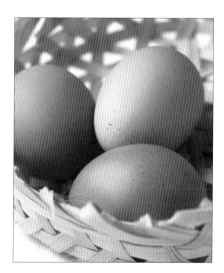

Baking ingredients

Some of the best-loved breads, cakes and biscuits (cookies) that we enjoy today are based on ancient traditional recipes. Early civilizations cooked flat, unleavened bread made simply from ground grains and water, and subsequently baking developed through the centuries with the addition of yeast to make leavened loaves. The first cakes were simply bread dough with added eggs or butter; many country cakes also contained fruit, nuts and seeds gathered wild from the hedgerows. Before commercially refined sugar was available, honey was used to sweeten baked goods. Many recipes for substantial country fruit cakes make the most of rather meagre ingredients, using very little flour, sugar and eggs with plenty of fruit and nuts, which gives a dark, moist cake that has a long storage life.

Unlike much country cooking, baking is based on careful attention to the amounts of each ingredient, and most recipes for cakes and bread rely on measuring by weight or by cup and spoon measures. Most baking also requires specific types of key basic ingredients such as flour. Strong bread flour, for instance, should only be used for baking bread, never cakes.

Like much that is best in country cooking, many rural baking recipes can be time-consuming to prepare, but the flavour and texture of a light home-made sponge cake or a tasty wholemeal (whole-wheat) loaf is well worth the effort.

Bread and cakes

Using only a few ingredients and with very simple equipment, bread-making was a skill which every traditional country cook needed to acquire. Although bread at its simplest is just flour, water, yeast and a little salt and sugar, many country breads are made with numerous other additions, including wholemeal flour, grains such as rye and barley, and oats or seeds added for extra texture and flavour.

Above *There are many types of flour and they are not interchangeable – use the correct one to suit the recipe.*

Through necessity, many peasant breads dispense with the need for yeast altogether. These include Irish soda bread, Turkish simit, American cornbread and unleavened breads such as Indian chapatis and Mexican tortillas. The need for bread which would keep well throughout the dark winter months led to the flat crisp breads of Scandinavia, while German and Polish peasants baked dark rye bread with added treacle or molasses to give a dense, sustaining texture.

Most of the best-loved, so-called 'fancy breads' were made from the dough left over from a weekly bread baking, with the addition of eggs, sugar, fruit or nuts to make sweetened loaves. Speciality breads with added spices and fruit were often made for celebrations or festivals: many had symbolic relevance, such as English hot cross buns to mark the Easter holiday.

Country cakes tend to be rather substantial, and based on simple but delicious ingredients rather than the elaborate cream-filled confections typical of pâtisserie. Many traditional cakes have their origins rooted in rituals and

Left *Bread comes in a variety of shapes and colours, from dark fruity sweet loaves to the classic farmhouse plait.*

Left *Baking day was a regular country tradition, providing home-made cakes and muffins for the coming week.*

worship. The Chinese offered up round cakes at harvest time to honour a moon goddess, while the ancient Celts used cakes in rituals on the first day of spring.

All cultures developed their own versions of basic recipes, with home-made cakes in Eastern Europe tending to be darker, spicier and containing more fruit, while in the USA muffins are the ultimate portable breakfast. Plain, nutritious mixtures such as oatcakes were peasant standbys eaten in place of bread during lean times when wheat was scarce or expensive.

Biscuits, pastry and puddings

From tray-baked flapjacks to crumbly shortbread, biscuits and cookies offered a variety of sweet treats to supplement a basic diet. Many traditional country cooks had a weekly baking day when they made enough cakes and biscuits (as well as bread) to last throughout the rest of the week.

From the simplest plain biscuits made from flour, sugar and a little fat, to rich, chocolate and nut-studded American cookies, the inventive cook has always made use of whatever was available in order to enliven plain dough mixtures. Tray bakes or bar cakes, such as brownies and flapjacks, are easy to make and transport, and make a good addition to a lunch box or picnic.

Tarts, pies and puddings are emblematic of the country kitchen, and sum up the sort of comfort food that traditional cooking does best. Pastry is a simple mixture of flour and fat, and is the basis of many of the best-known savoury country recipes, such as quiches, pasties, flans and pies. Its sweet form comes in many variations, such as doughnuts or fried churros from Spain. Sweet pastry made with almonds is widely used in Italian, Spanish and Middle Eastern cooking, and the almond-stuffed Gateau de Roi is still the traditional Christmas pastry of Provence.

Steamed puddings were popular in the country because they do not require an oven. A sponge or suet (US chilled, grated shortening) mixture is gently steamed in a covered bowl on the hob for an hour or two. These substantial puddings, often containing fruit inside the pastry crust, only need the addition of a jug (pitcher) of creamy custard to make a delicious sweet treat.

Left A home-made harvest loaf, shaped like a wheatsheaf to celebrate the end of the harvest, symbolizes the importance of our 'daily bread'.
Right Baked desserts and cakes make the most of the fruits and other ingredients available in each season.

Soups and appetizers

A warming bowl of home-made soup with some crusty bread and a chunk of cheese is a staple lunch or supper, relying, like most country cooking, on good seasonal ingredients. Using a home-made stock makes all the difference. This chapter also includes some tasty ideas for appetizers, such as stuffed field mushrooms, flavoursome tarts and tartlets, and a wonderful gamekeeper's terrine.

Rustic mushroom soup

Using a mixture of mushrooms gives real depth of flavour to this soup – if you have some
wild mushrooms include them for extra character. Serve with cream and chopped parsley.

**Serves 4–6 as a light meal or
6–8 as a soup course**

20g/¾oz/1½ tbsp butter

15ml/1 tbsp oil

1 onion, roughly chopped

4 potatoes, about 250–350g/
9–12oz, roughly chopped

350g/12oz mixed mushrooms,
such as Paris Browns,
field (portabello) and
button (white)

1 or 2 garlic cloves, crushed

150ml/¼ pint/⅔ cup white
wine or dry (hard) cider

1.2 litres/2 pints/5 cups
good chicken stock

bunch of fresh parsley, chopped

salt and ground black pepper

whipped or sour cream, to garnish

◄ **1** Heat the butter and oil in a large
pan, over medium heat. Add the onion
and potatoes. Cover and sweat over a
low heat for 5–10 minutes until softened
but not browned. Chop the mushrooms.

2 Add the mushrooms, garlic and white
wine or cider and stock. Season, bring
to the boil and cook for 15 minutes,
until all the ingredients are tender.

3 Put the mixture through a mouli-
légumes (food mill), using the coarse
blade, or liquidize (blend). Return
the soup to the rinsed pan, and add
three-quarters of the parsley. Bring back
to the boil, season, and garnish with
cream and the remaining parsley.

Per portion Energy 155kcal/648kJ; Protein 3.3g; Carbohydrate 13.6g, of which sugars 3.4g; Fat 7.6g, of which saturates 3.1g; Cholesterol 11mg; Calcium 23mg; Fibre 2.1g; Sodium 117mg.

Garlic soup

This subtly flavoured, aromatic soup is best made with plenty of fresh garlic and good stock
– a French traditional soup that is not only delicious but very healthy too.

Serves 8

12 large garlic cloves, peeled

15ml/1 tbsp olive oil

15ml/1 tbsp melted butter

1 small onion, finely chopped

15g/½oz/2 tbsp plain
(all-purpose) flour

15ml/1 tbsp white wine vinegar

1 litre/1¾ pints/4 cups
chicken stock

2 egg yolks, lightly beaten

bread croûtons, fried in
butter, to serve

1 Crush the garlic. Put the oil and butter
into a pan, add the garlic and onion, and
cook them gently for 20 minutes.

2 Add the flour and stir to make a roux.
Cook for a few minutes, then stir in the
wine vinegar, stock and 1 litre/1¾ pints/
4 cups water. Simmer for 30 minutes.

3 When ready to serve, whisk in the
egg yolks and do not allow the soup to
boil again. Put the croûtons into soup
bowls and pour the hot soup over.

Cook's tip This garlic soup brings a
great sense of well-being and is a real
treat for garlic-lovers.

Per portion Energy 55kcal/229kJ; Protein 1.3g; Carbohydrate 3g, of which sugars 0.5g; Fat 4.4g, of which saturates 1.6g; Cholesterol 54mg; Calcium 12mg; Fibre 0.3g; Sodium 50mg.

Parsnip soup

This is a spicy winter country soup. It can also be made with other root vegetables, such as carrots or celeriac. It is delicious garnished with parsnip crisps or fried garlic croûtons.

Serves 6

900g/2lb parsnips

50g/2oz/¼ cup butter

1 onion, chopped

2 garlic cloves, crushed

10ml/2 tsp ground cumin

5ml/1 tsp ground coriander

about 1.2 litres/2 pints/5 cups hot chicken stock

150ml/¼ pint/⅔ cup single (light) cream

salt and ground black pepper

chopped fresh chives or parsley and/or croûtons, to garnish

1 Peel and thinly slice the parsnips. Heat the butter in a large heavy pan and add the peeled parsnips and chopped onion with the crushed garlic. Cook until softened, stirring occasionally.

2 Add the cumin and coriander to the vegetable mixture and cook, stirring, for 1–2 minutes, then gradually blend in the hot chicken stock and mix well.

3 Cover and simmer for about 20 minutes, or until the parsnip is soft. Purée the soup, adjust the texture with extra stock or water if it seems too thick, and check the seasoning. Add the cream and reheat without boiling.

4 Serve immediately, sprinkled with chopped chives or parsley and/or croûtons, to garnish.

Per portion Energy 215kcal/899kJ; Protein 3.9g; Carbohydrate 21.3g, of which sugars 10.6g; Fat 13.3g, of which saturates 7.7g; Cholesterol 32mg; Calcium 92mg; Fibre 7.3g; Sodium 74mg.

Leek and potato soup

A hearty winter classic, this soup is full of chunky vegetables. If you prefer a smooth version, press the soup through a sieve and finish with crème fraîche and sliced fried leeks.

Serves 4

50g/2oz/¼ cup butter

2 leeks, washed and chopped

1 small onion, peeled and finely chopped

350g/12oz potatoes, peeled and chopped

900ml/1½ pints/3¾ cups chicken or vegetable stock

salt and ground black pepper

chopped fresh parsley, to garnish

1 Heat 25g/1oz/2 tbsp of the butter in a large pan over a medium heat. Add the leeks and onion and cook gently, stirring occasionally, for about 7 minutes, until they are softened but not browned.

Cook's tips
• Don't use a food processor to purée this soup as it can give the potatoes a gluey consistency. The potatoes should be left to crumble and disintegrate naturally as they boil, making the consistency of the soup thicker the longer you leave them.
• If you can, make your own chicken or vegetable stock by simmering bones and vegetables in water for 2 hours and straining the liquid.

2 Add the potatoes to the pan and cook for about 2–3 minutes, then add the stock and bring to the boil. Cover and simmer for 30–35 minutes.

3 Season to taste and remove the pan from the heat. Dice and stir in the remaining butter. Garnish with the chopped parsley and serve hot.

Per portion Energy 179kcal/747kJ; Protein 3.2g; Carbohydrate 17.9g, of which sugars 4g; Fat 11g, of which saturates 6.7g; Cholesterol 27mg; Calcium 32mg; Fibre 3g; Sodium 88mg.

Country tomato soup

This creamy soup owes its great flavour to a generous mix of fresh and canned tomatoes, but in the summer it can be made with all ripe sweet and fragrant fresh tomatoes from the vine and garnished with a few fresh basil leaves from the kitchen garden.

Serves 4–6

25g/1oz/2 tbsp butter

1 medium onion, finely chopped

1 small carrot, finely chopped

1 celery stick, finely chopped

1 garlic clove, crushed

450g/1lb ripe tomatoes, roughly chopped

400g/14oz can chopped tomatoes

30ml/2 tbsp tomato purée (paste)

30ml/2 tbsp sugar

15ml/1 tbsp chopped fresh thyme or oregano leaves

600ml/1 pint/2½ cups chicken or vegetable stock

600ml/1 pint/2½ cups milk

salt and ground black pepper

1 Melt the butter in a large pan. Add the onion, carrot, celery and garlic. Cook over a medium heat for about 5 minutes, stirring occasionally, until soft and just beginning to brown. Add the tomatoes, purée, sugar, stock and herbs, retaining some to garnish.

2 Bring to the boil, then cover and simmer gently for about 20 minutes until all the vegetables are very soft. Process or blend the mixture until smooth, then press it through a sieve (strainer) to remove the skins and seeds, which can be discarded.

3 Return the sieved (strained) soup to the cleaned pan and stir in the milk. Reheat gently.

4 Stir, without allowing it to boil. Season with salt and pepper. Garnish with the remaining herbs and serve.

Per portion Energy 107kcal/447kJ; Protein 2.3g; Carbohydrate 11.4g, of which sugars 10.9g; Fat 6.1g, of which saturates 3.5g; Cholesterol 13mg; Calcium 50mg; Fibre 3.9g; Sodium 71mg.

Chunky country vegetable soup

Soup-making is an excellent way of making the most of fresh seasonal vegetables just harvested from the garden. This substantial soup makes a hearty appetizer or a satisfying light meal, and goes well with chunks of crusty bread and wedges of cheese.

Serves 6

15ml/1 tbsp oil

25g/1oz/2 tbsp butter

2 medium onions, finely chopped

4 medium carrots, sliced

2 celery sticks, sliced

2 leeks, sliced

1 potato, cut into small cubes

1 small parsnip, cut into small cubes

1 garlic clove, crushed

900ml/1½ pints/3¾ cups vegetable stock

300ml/½ pint/1¼ cups milk

25g/1oz/4 tbsp cornflour (cornstarch)

handful of frozen peas

30ml/2 tbsp chopped fresh parsley

salt and ground black pepper

2 Add the stock to the pan and stir into the vegetables. Bring the mixture slowly to the boil, cover and simmer gently for 20–30 minutes until all the vegetables are tender but not too soft.

3 Whisk the milk into the cornflour, making a paste. Stir into the vegetables. Add the frozen peas. Bring to the boil and simmer for 5 minutes. Adjust the seasoning, stir in the parsley and serve.

1 Heat the oil and butter in a large pan and add the onions, carrots and celery. Cook over a medium heat for 5–10 minutes, stirring occasionally, until soft and just beginning to turn golden brown. Add the leeks, potato, parsnip and garlic and stir well together.

Per portion Energy 160kcal/665kJ; Protein 3.6g; Carbohydrate 11.5g, of which sugars 10g; Fat 11.4g, of which saturates 6.8g; Cholesterol 27mg; Calcium 72mg; Fibre 5.4g; Sodium 106mg.

Bacon and barley broth

Use a good-sized bacon hock to flavour this soup, which is thick with barley and lentils. Hearty peasant cooking makes this a nutritious and comforting soup.

Serves 6–8

1 bacon hock, about 900g/2lb

75g/3oz/⅓ cup pearl barley

75g/3oz/⅓ cup lentils

2 leeks, sliced, or onions, diced

4 carrots, diced

200g/7oz swede (rutabaga), diced

3 potatoes, diced

small bunch of herbs (thyme, parsley, bay leaf)

1 small cabbage, trimmed, quartered or sliced

salt and ground black pepper

chopped fresh parsley, to garnish

brown bread, to serve

Cook's tip Traditionally, the cabbage is simply trimmed and quartered, although it may be thinly sliced or shredded, if you prefer.

1 Soak the bacon in cold water overnight. Next morning, drain it and put it into a large pan with enough fresh cold water to cover it. Bring to the boil, skim off any scum that rises to the surface, and then add the barley and lentils. Bring back to the boil and simmer for about 15 minutes.

2 Add the vegetables to the pan with some black pepper and the herbs. Bring back to the boil, reduce the heat and simmer gently for 1½ hours, or until the meat is tender.

3 Lift the bacon hock from the pan with a slotted spoon. Remove the skin, then take the meat off the bones and break it into bitesize pieces. Return to the pan with the cabbage. Discard the herbs and cook for a little longer until the cabbage is cooked to your liking.

4 Adjust the seasoning and ladle into large serving bowls, garnish with parsley and serve with freshly baked brown bread.

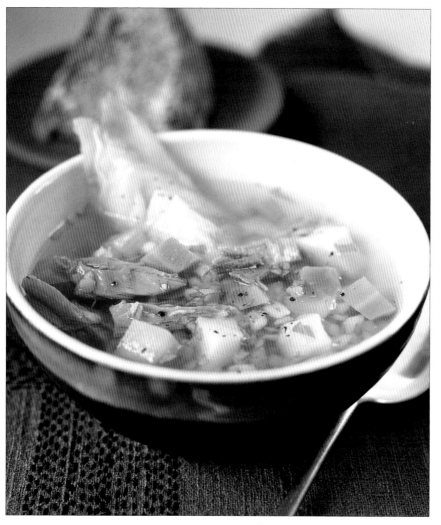

Per portion Energy 306kcal/1284kJ; Protein 17.7g; Carbohydrate 33.5g, of which sugars 8.3g; Fat 12.1g, of which saturates 4.3g; Cholesterol 35mg; Calcium 74mg; Fibre 4.6g; Sodium 1.05g.

Lamb and vegetable broth

A contemporary version of the classic Irish mutton soup, this meaty broth includes lots of winter vegetables. It is very tasty served with chunks of Irish soda bread.

Serves 6

675g/1½lb neck of lamb (US shoulder or breast) on the bone

1 large onion

2 bay leaves

3 carrots, chopped

½ white turnip, diced

½ small white cabbage, shredded

2 large leeks, thinly sliced

15ml/1 tbsp tomato purée (paste)

30ml/2 tbsp chopped fresh parsley

salt and ground black pepper

1 Trim any excess fat from the meat. Chop the onion, and put the lamb and bay leaves in a large pan. Add 1.5 litres/ 2½ pints/6¼ cups water and bring to the boil. Skim the surface and then simmer for about 1½–2 hours. Remove the lamb on to a board and leave to cool until ready to handle.

2 Remove the meat from the bones and cut into small pieces. Discard the bones and return the meat to the broth. Add the vegetables, tomato purée and parsley, and season well. Simmer for another 30 minutes, until the vegetables are tender. Ladle into soup bowls and serve.

Per portion Energy 162kcal/675kJ; Protein 13.1g; Carbohydrate 8.5g, of which sugars 7g; Fat 8.6g, of which saturates 3.8g; Cholesterol 44mg; Calcium 42mg; Fibre 3g; Sodium 55mg.

Beef and split pea broth

A restorative and nutritious meaty broth that will taste even more delicious when reheated, this hearty country soup will warm and comfort on a dark winter evening.

Serves 6–8

450–675g/1–1½lb rib steak, or other stewing beef on the bone

2 large onions

50g/2oz/¼ cup pearl barley

50g/2oz/¼ cup green split peas

3 large carrots, chopped

2 white turnips, peeled and chopped into dice

3 celery stalks, chopped

1 large or 2 medium leeks, thinly sliced and washed in cold water

sea salt and ground black pepper

chopped fresh parsley, to serve

1 Bone the meat and put the bones and half an onion, roughly sliced, into a large pan. Cover with cold water, season with salt and pepper, and bring to the boil. Skim if necessary, then simmer until needed.

2 Meanwhile, trim any fat or gristle from the meat and cut into small pieces. Chop the remaining onions finely with a sharp knife.

3 Drain the stock from the bones, make it up with water to 2 litres/3½ pints/ 9 cups, and return to the rinsed pan with the meat, onions, barley and split peas.

4 Season, bring to the boil, and skim if necessary. Reduce the heat, cover and simmer for about 30 minutes.

5 Add the carrots, turnip, celery and leeks to the pan and simmer for a further 1 hour, or until the meat is tender. Check the seasoning and adjust if necessary.

6 Serve the soup immediately in large individual warmed bowls, generously sprinkled with the chopped parsley.

Per portion Energy 167kcal/705kJ; Protein 16g; Carbohydrate 21.4g, of which sugars 7.8g; Fat 2.6g, of which saturates 0.8g; Cholesterol 34mg; Calcium 54mg; Fibre 3.6g; Sodium 58mg.

Oxtail soup

Frugal country cooks utilize every part of an animal. Even the cheapest cuts respond well to slow cooking – oxtail becomes rich, dark and tender when slow cooked.

Serves 4–6

1 oxtail, cut into joints, total weight about 1.3kg/3lb

25g/1oz/2 tbsp butter

2 medium onions, chopped

2 medium carrots, chopped

2 celery sticks, sliced

1 bacon rasher (strip), chopped

2 litres/3½ pints/8 cups beef stock

1 bouquet garni

2 bay leaves

30ml/2 tbsp flour

squeeze of fresh lemon juice

60ml/4 tbsp port, sherry or Madeira

salt and ground black pepper

1 Wash and dry the pieces of oxtail, trimming off any excess fat. Melt the butter in a large pan, and when foaming, add the oxtail a few pieces at a time and brown them quickly on all sides. Lift the meat out on to a plate.

2 To the same pan, add the onions, carrots, celery and bacon. Cook over a medium heat for 5–10 minutes, stirring, until the vegetables are softened.

3 Return the oxtail to the pan and add the stock, bouquet garni, bay leaves and seasoning. Bring just to the boil and skim off any foam. Cover and simmer gently for about 3 hours or until the meat is so tender that it is falling away from the bones.

4 Strain the mixture, discarding the vegetables, bouquet garni and bay leaves, and leave to stand.

5 When the oxtail has cooled sufficiently to handle, pick all the meat off the bones and cut it into small pieces.

6 Skim off any fat that has risen to the surface of the stock, then transfer the stock into a large pan. Add the pieces of meat and reheat.

7 With a whisk, blend the flour with a little cold water to make a smooth paste. Stir in a little of the hot stock, then stir the mixture into the pan. Bring to the boil, stirring, until the soup thickens slightly. Reduce the heat and simmer gently for about 5 minutes.

8 Season with salt, pepper and lemon juice to taste. Just before serving, stir in the port, sherry or Madeira.

Per portion Energy 459kcal/1914kJ; Protein 45.4g; Carbohydrate 6.5g, of which sugars 2.6g; Fat 26.8g, of which saturates 11.8g; Cholesterol 176mg; Calcium 36mg; Fibre 0.7g; Sodium 403mg.

Field mushrooms stuffed with hazelnuts

Meaty field mushrooms filled with an aromatic mix of garlic and parley and topped with crunchy chopped hazelnuts make a delicious vegetarian appetizer or side dish.

Serves 4

2 garlic cloves

grated rind of 1 lemon

90ml/6 tbsp olive oil

8 large field (portabello) mushrooms

50g/2oz/½ cup hazelnuts, coarsely chopped

30ml/2 tbsp chopped fresh parsley

salt and ground black pepper

1 Crush the garlic cloves with a little salt. Place in a bowl and stir in the grated lemon rind and the olive oil. If time allows, leave to infuse (steep).

2 Preheat the oven to 200°C/400°F/ Gas 6. Arrange the field mushrooms, stalk side up, in a single layer in an ovenproof earthenware dish.

3 Drizzle over about 60ml/4 tbsp of the oil mixture and bake in the oven for about 10 minutes.

4 Remove the mushrooms from the oven and baste them with the remaining oil mixture, then sprinkle the chopped hazelnuts evenly over the top.

5 Bake for a further 10–15 minutes, or until the mushrooms are tender. Season with salt and pepper and sprinkle with chopped parsley. Serve immediately.

Cook's tip Almost any unsalted nuts can be used in place of the hazelnuts in this recipe – try pine nuts, cashew nuts, almonds or walnuts. Nuts can go rancid quickly so, for the freshest flavour, either buy nuts in small quantities or buy them in shells and remove the shells just before use.

Per portion Energy 255kcal/1052kJ; Protein 5.2g; Carbohydrate 1.7g, of which sugars 1g; Fat 25.4g, of which saturates 3.1g; Cholesterol 0mg; Calcium 43mg; Fibre 3.1g; Sodium 12mg.

Wild mushroom and sun-dried tomato soufflés

Foraged wild mushrooms would be ideal for this recipe. These delightful soufflés are remarkably easy to prepare, and are perfect either as an appetizer or light lunch.

Serves 4

25g/1oz/½ cup dried
cep mushrooms

40g/1½oz/3 tbsp butter, plus extra
for greasing

20ml/4 tsp grated Parmesan cheese

40g/1½oz/⅓ cup plain
(all-purpose) flour

250ml/8fl oz/1 cup milk

50g/2oz/½ cup grated mature (sharp)
Cheddar cheese

4 eggs, separated

2 sun-dried tomatoes in oil, drained
and chopped

15ml/1 tbsp chopped fresh chives

salt and ground black pepper

Cook's tip A variety of different dried mushrooms are available – any can be used instead of the ceps.

1 Place the ceps in a bowl, pour over enough warm water to cover and leave to soak for 15 minutes. Grease four individual earthenware soufflé dishes with a little butter.

2 Sprinkle the grated Parmesan cheese into the soufflé dishes and rotate each dish to coat the sides with cheese. Preheat the oven to 190°C/375°F/Gas 5.

3 Melt the 40g/1½oz/3 tbsp of butter in a large pan, remove from the heat and stir in the flour. Cook over a low heat for 1 minute, stirring constantly. Remove the pan from the heat and gradually stir in the milk. Return to the heat and bring to the boil, stirring constantly, until the sauce has thickened.

4 Remove the sauce from the heat, then stir in the grated Cheddar cheese and plenty of seasoning. Beat in the egg yolks, one at a time, then stir in the chopped sun-dried tomatoes and the chives. Drain the soaked mushrooms, then coarsely chop them and add them to the cheese sauce.

5 Whisk the egg whites until they stand in soft peaks. Mix one spoonful into the sauce, then carefully fold in the remainder. Divide the mixture among the soufflé dishes and bake for 25 minutes, or until the soufflés are golden brown on top, well risen and just firm to the touch. Serve immediately – before they sink.

Per portion Energy 290kcal/1207kJ; Protein 14.7g; Carbohydrate 11.6g, of which sugars 3.9g; Fat 20.8g, of which saturates 11.2g; Cholesterol 232mg; Calcium 274mg; Fibre 0.6g; Sodium 305mg.

Savoury leek and onion tarts

Leeks are a great winter vegetable, and when combined with sliced onion and grated Gruyére cheese, these tarts make a good addition to a picnic, buffet or a vegetarian lunch.

Serves 6

25g/1oz/2 tbsp butter, plus extra for greasing

1 onion, thinly sliced

2.5ml/½ tsp dried thyme

450g/1lb/4 cups leeks, thinly sliced

50g/2oz/½ cup Gruyère cheese, grated

3 eggs

300ml/½ pint/1¼ cups single (light) cream

pinch of freshly grated nutmeg

salt and ground black pepper

mixed salad leaves, to serve

For the pastry

175g/6oz/1½ cups plain (all-purpose) flour

75g/3oz/6 tbsp cold butter

1 egg yolk

30–45ml/2–3 tbsp cold water

2.5ml/½ tsp salt

1 To make the pastry, sift the flour into a large bowl and add the cold butter. Using your hands, gently rub the butter into the flour until the mixture resembles fine breadcrumbs.

2 Make a well in the flour mixture. Beat together the egg yolk, water and salt. Pour into the well and mix lightly to form a stiff dough. Form into a flattened ball. Wrap and chill for 30 minutes.

3 Butter six 10cm/4in tartlet tins (muffin pans). On a lightly floured surface, roll out the dough until 3mm/⅛in thick then, using a 12.5cm/5in cutter, cut as many rounds as possible. Ease the rounds into the tins, pressing the pastry firmly into the base and sides. Reroll the trimmings and line the remaining tins. Prick the bases and chill for 30 minutes.

4 Preheat the oven to 190°C/375°F/Gas 5. Line the pastry cases with foil and fill with baking beans. Place them on a baking sheet and bake for 6–8 minutes until golden at the edges.

5 Remove the foil and beans, and bake for 2 minutes until the bases appear dry. Transfer to a wire rack to cool. Reduce the oven temperature to 180°C/350°F/Gas 4.

6 In a large frying pan, melt the butter over a medium heat, then add the onion and thyme, and cook for 3–5 minutes until the onion is just softened, stirring frequently. Add the leeks and cook for 10–12 minutes until they are soft and tender. Divide the mixture among the pastry cases and sprinkle each with cheese, dividing it evenly.

7 In a medium bowl, beat the eggs, cream, nutmeg and salt and pepper. Place the pastry cases on a baking sheet and pour on the egg mixture.

8 Bake for 15–20 minutes until set and golden. Transfer the tartlets to a wire rack to cool slightly, then remove them from the tins and serve warm or at room temperature with a selection of fresh salad leaves.

Per portion Energy 422kcal/1755kJ; Protein 11.5g; Carbohydrate 26.8g, of which sugars 3.9g; Fat 30.4g, of which saturates 17.7g; Cholesterol 200mg; Calcium 189mg; Fibre 2.7g; Sodium 215mg.

Feta and olive tartlets

Delicious for lunch or a snack, these crisp little tarts showcase the best Mediterranean flavours. They freeze well and can be stuffed with a variety of fillings.

Serves 4

25g/1oz sun-dried aubergine (eggplant) slices

300ml/½ pint/1¼ cups boiling water

45ml/3 tbsp sunflower oil

1 onion, thinly sliced

150g/5oz/2 cups button (white) mushrooms, sliced

1 garlic clove, crushed

12–16 cherry tomatoes, halved

8 black or green olives, pitted and chopped

115g/4oz/1 cup feta cheese, crumbled

350g/12oz ready-made puff pastry

salt and ground black pepper

1 Preheat the oven to 200°C/400°F/ Gas 6. Place the aubergine slices in a shallow dish. Pour over the boiling water and leave to soak for 10 minutes. Rinse in cold water, drain and dry on kitchen paper. Cut the aubergine slices in half or quarters, depending on their size.

Cook's tip Choose cherry tomatoes on the vine or some semi-dried sun blush tomatoes for the very best flavour in these tartlets.

2 Heat 30ml/2 tbsp of the sunflower oil in a frying pan and fry the onion over a medium heat for 4–5 minutes. Add the mushrooms and cook for 3–4 minutes, or until the onions are light golden. Remove and set aside.

3 Heat the remaining oil in the frying pan, add the aubergine slices and garlic and lightly fry for 1–2 minutes. Lightly oil four individual clay pots. Mix the halved tomatoes with the onions, mushrooms, aubergines, olives and feta cheese and divide among the clay pots. Season well.

4 Roll out the pastry thinly into an oblong, then cut out four rounds, each slightly larger than the diameter of the clay pots.

5 Place the pastry rounds on top of the vegetable and cheese mixture, tucking any overlapping pastry down inside the dish.

6 Bake the tarts for about 20 minutes, or until the pastry is risen and golden. Allow to cool slightly, then carefully invert on to individual warmed serving plates to serve.

Per portion Energy 506kcal/2105kJ; Protein 11.1g; Carbohydrate 35.9g, of which sugars 4.1g; Fat 37.2g, of which saturates 5.2g; Cholesterol 20mg; Calcium 175mg; Fibre 1.6g; Sodium 989mg.

Gamekeeper's terrine

Hare and other furred game are popular in country cooking, having been hunted as food for centuries. For tender meat and a good flavour, use young hare that has been hung for at least a week. Rabbit would also be delicious in this terrine, or a mixture of minced pork and rabbit meat. Make sure you have plenty of hot toast to serve with it.

Serves 4–6

5 dried mushrooms, rinsed and soaked in warm water for 30 minutes

saddle, thighs, liver, heart and lungs of 1 hare

2 onions, cut into wedges

1 carrot, chopped

1 parsnip, chopped

4 bay leaves

10 allspice berries

300g/11oz calf's liver

165g/5½oz unsmoked streaky (fatty) bacon rashers (strips)

75g/3oz/1½ cups soft white breadcrumbs

4 eggs

105ml/7 tbsp 95 per cent proof Polish spirit or vodka

5ml/1 tsp freshly grated nutmeg

10ml/2 tsp dried marjoram

10g/¼oz juniper berries

4 garlic cloves, crushed

150g/5oz smoked streaky (fatty) bacon rashers (strips)

salt and ground black pepper, to taste

redcurrant jelly and salad, to serve

Cook's tip To make sure the bacon doesn't shrink during cooking, stretch each rasher (strip) out thinly on a board with the back of a knife.

1 Drain the mushrooms and slice into strips. Put the pieces of hare in a large pan and pour in enough water to just cover. Add the onions, carrot, parsnip, mushrooms, bay leaves and allspice.

2 Bring to the boil, then cover and simmer gently for 1 hour. Add a pinch of salt and allow the meat to cool in the stock.

3 Slice the liver and 50g/2oz unsmoked bacon into small pieces and put in a medium pan. Add a ladleful of the stock and simmer for 15 minutes.

4 Preheat the oven to 180°C/350°F/ Gas 4. Put two ladlefuls of the stock in a small bowl, add the breadcrumbs and leave to soak.

5 Remove the hare pieces, liver and bacon from the stock and chop finely with a large knife.

6 Transfer to a large bowl, then add the soaked breadcrumbs, eggs, Polish spirit or vodka, nutmeg, marjoram, juniper berries and crushed garlic. Season to taste and mix well to combine thoroughly.

7 Line a 1.2 litre/2 pint/5 cup ovenproof dish with the smoked and remaining unsmoked bacon rashers, making sure they overhang the edges. Spoon in the meat mixture and bring the overhanging bacon over the top. Cover with buttered baking parchment, then cover with a lid or foil.

8 Place the dish in a roasting pan containing boiling water, then put in the oven and bake for 1½ hours, or until a skewer pushed into the centre comes out clean and the juices run clear. Remove the baking parchment and lid or foil about 15 minutes before the end of cooking to allow the terrine to brown.

9 Remove from the oven, and take the dish out of the roasting pan. Cover the terrine with baking parchment and a board and weight down with a 900g/2lb weight (such as two cans). Leave to cool, then turn out on to a serving dish. Serve in slices with redcurrant jelly and a green salad.

Per portion Energy 266kcal/1112kJ; Protein 27.1g; Carbohydrate 6.4g, of which sugars 1.4g; Fat 14g, of which saturates 5g; Cholesterol 182mg; Calcium 25mg; Fibre 0.3g; Sodium 432mg.

Fish and shellfish

Steamed, grilled or barbecued, fish and shellfish are
the ultimate fast food. More elaborate dishes
originate from the practical needs of fisher folk –
after selling the prime catch, the leftover small or
ugly fish would be included in tasty and filling stews,
transforming them into delicious and nutritious
meals. Many cultures share the same basic fish
recipes, which can be adapted to include whichever
types of fish are available at the time.

Haddock in cider sauce

Both smoked and unsmoked, haddock is a popular fish that finds its way into many traditional country dishes. It is a firm, meaty fish, so is beautifully complemented by the well-flavoured dry cider sauce in this recipe. New potatoes, carrots and mangetouts are perfect accompaniments, together with a garnish of sliced apple sautéed in butter.

Serves 4

675g/1½lb haddock fillet

1 medium onion, thinly sliced

1 bay leaf

2 sprigs fresh parsley

10ml/2 tsp lemon juice

450ml/¾ pint/2 cups dry (hard) cider

25g/1oz/¼ cup cornflour (cornstarch)

30ml/2 tbsp single (light) cream

salt and ground black pepper

1 Cut the haddock fillet into four equal portions and place in a pan big enough to hold them neatly in a single layer. Add the onion, bay leaf, parsley and lemon juice, and season with salt.

2 Pour in most of the cider, reserving 30ml/2 tbsp for the sauce. Cover and bring to the boil, reduce the heat and simmer for 10 minutes, or until the fish is just cooked.

3 Strain 300ml/½ pint/1¼ cups of the fish liquor into a measuring jug (cup). In a small pan, mix the cornflour with the reserved cider, then gradually whisk in the fish liquor and bring to the boil, whisking constantly for about 2 minutes, until it is smooth and thickened. Add more of the cooking liquor, if necessary, to make a pouring sauce. Remove the pan from the heat, stir in the single cream and season to taste with salt and freshly ground black pepper.

4 To serve, remove any skin from the fish, arrange on individual hot serving plates with the onion over the vegetables and pour the sauce over.

Per portion Energy 227kcal/964kJ; Protein 32.8g; Carbohydrate 11.8g, of which sugars 5.2g; Fat 2.6g, of which saturates 1.1g; Cholesterol 65mg; Calcium 50mg; Fibre 0.5g; Sodium 128mg.

West coast fisherman's stew

The location in the title of this recipe refers to the little ports along the west coast of Scotland, places where fishermen land small catches of monkfish, haddock, prawns and crabs. This recipe uses whatever fish and shellfish appear in the catch of the day. Use your favourite fish and vary the shellfish – clams, mussels, prawns or crayfish all work well.

Serves 4

30ml/2 tbsp olive oil

1 large onion, roughly chopped

1 leek, roughly chopped

2 garlic cloves, crushed

450g/1lb ripe tomatoes, roughly chopped

5ml/1 tsp tomato purée (paste)

1.3kg/3lb fish bones

a piece of pared orange peel

a few parsley stalks and fennel fronds

1 bay leaf

250ml/8fl oz/1 cup dry white wine

whisky or pastis, such as Pernod (optional)

1kg/2¼lb mixed fish fillets, such as salmon, sole and haddock, cut into chunks, and prepared shellfish

salt and ground black pepper

chopped fresh parsley, to garnish

1 Heat the olive oil in a large pan, then sweat the onion and leek until soft. Add the garlic, tomatoes and tomato purée, and cook for 5 minutes.

2 Put in the fish bones, orange peel, herbs and wine, and add a little salt and ground black pepper. Then add enough water just to cover. Bring to a gentle boil, then reduce the heat and simmer for 30 minutes.

3 Strain the soup into a clean pan, pressing the juices out of the solid ingredients with the back of a spoon.

4 Bring the liquid back to the boil and check for seasoning and texture. If you like, add a splash of whisky or Pernod. The fish takes just minutes to cook so add the firmer, larger pieces first, such as monkfish or salmon and mussels in the shell, and end with delicate scallops or prawn (shrimp) tails. Do not allow the stew to boil once you add the fish.

5 Serve in warmed soup plates, garnished with chopped fresh parsley.

Per portion Energy 341kcal/1432kJ; Protein 47.5g; Carbohydrate 6.5g, of which sugars 5.8g; Fat 7.8g, of which saturates 1.2g; Cholesterol 115mg; Calcium 53mg; Fibre 2.3g; Sodium 165mg.

Cod and bean casserole with saffron and paprika

It's sometimes nice to dine away from the table, and this is just the no-nonsense dish to do it with. With everything cooked in one pot, this appetizing casserole with chunks of fresh, flaky cod can be served simply with hunks of crusty bread and a crisp green side salad.

Serves 6–8

1 large red (bell) pepper

45ml/3 tbsp olive oil

4 rashers (strips) streaky (fatty) bacon, roughly chopped

4 garlic cloves, finely chopped

1 onion, sliced

10ml/2 tsp paprika

5ml/1 tsp hot pimentón (smoked Spanish paprika)

large pinch of saffron threads or 1 sachet powdered saffron, soaked in 45ml/3 tbsp hot water

400g/14oz jar Spanish butter (lima) beans (judias del barco or judias blancas guisadas) or canned haricot (navy) beans, drained and rinsed

about 600ml/1 pint/2½ cups fish stock, or water and 60ml/4 tbsp Thai fish sauce

6 plum tomatoes, quartered

350g/12oz fresh skinned cod fillet, cut into large chunks

45ml/3 tbsp chopped fresh coriander (cilantro), plus a few sprigs to garnish

salt and ground black pepper

crusty bread, to serve

1 Preheat the grill (broiler) and line the pan with foil. Halve the red pepper and scoop out the seeds.

2 Place the red pepper, cut-side down, in the grill pan and grill (broil) under a hot heat for about 10–15 minutes, until the skin is black and charred.

3 Put the pepper into a plastic bag, seal and leave for 10 minutes to steam, which will make the skin easier to remove.

4 Remove the pepper from the bag, peel and chop into large pieces.

5 Heat the olive oil in a pan, then add the chopped streaky bacon and the chopped garlic. Fry for about 2 minutes, then add the sliced onion.

6 Cover the pan and cook for about another 5 minutes until the onion is soft. Stir in the paprika and pimentón, the saffron and its soaking water, and salt and pepper.

7 Stir the beans into the pan and add just enough of the stock to cover them. Bring to the boil and simmer, uncovered, for about 15 minutes, stirring occasionally to prevent it from sticking.

8 Stir in the chopped pepper and tomato quarters. Drop in the cubes of cod and bury them in the sauce.

9 Cover and simmer for 5 minutes until the fish is cooked. Stir in the chopped coriander.

10 Divide the stew equally between six to eight warmed soup plates or bowls, garnishing each one with the coriander sprigs. Serve with lots of crusty bread.

Cook's tip If you prefer to use dried beans, soak them in water for 12 hours or overnight, rinse and then boil for 40–50 minutes depending on the beans.

Per portion Energy 449kcal/1883kJ; Protein 44.5g; Carbohydrate 25.3g, of which sugars 3.9g; Fat 19.5g, of which saturates 3g; Cholesterol 84mg; Calcium 85mg; Fibre 9.8g; Sodium 403mg.

Fresh mackerel with gooseberry relish

Packed with beneficial oils, fresh mackerel is not only tasty but also nutritionally rich. The tart gooseberries in this recipe are good for you too, as well as being a perfect accompaniment to any type of oily fish, including salmon and sardines.

Serves 4

4 whole mackerel

60ml/4 tbsp olive oil

For the sauce

250g/9oz gooseberries

25g/1oz/2 tbsp soft light brown sugar

5ml/1 tsp wholegrain mustard

salt and ground black pepper

1 For the sauce, wash and trim the gooseberries and then roughly chop them, so there are some pieces larger than others.

2 Cook the gooseberries in a little water with the sugar in a small pan. A thick and chunky purée will form. Add the mustard and season to taste with salt and ground black pepper.

Cook's tips
• Turn the grill (broiler) on well in advance as the fish need a fierce heat to cook quickly. If you like the fish but hate the smell, try barbecuing outside.
• The foil lining in the grill pan is to catch the smelly drips. Simply roll it up and throw it away afterwards, leaving a nice clean grill pan.

3 Preheat the grill (broiler) to high and line the grill pan with foil. Using a sharp knife, slash the fish two or three times down each side, then season and brush with the olive oil.

4 Place the fish in the grill pan and grill (broil) for about 4 minutes on each side until cooked. You may need to cook them for a few minutes longer if they are particularly large. The slashes will open up to speed cooking and the skin should be lightly browned. To check that they are cooked properly, use a small sharp knife to pierce the skin and check for uncooked flesh.

5 Place the mackerel on warmed plates and spread generous dollops of the gooseberry relish over them. Pass the remaining sauce around at the table.

Per portion Energy 576kcal/2390kJ; Protein 38.1g; Carbohydrate 8.4g, of which sugars 8.4g; Fat 43.5g, of which saturates 8.2g; Cholesterol 108mg; Calcium 43mg; Fibre 1.5g; Sodium 128mg.

Chunky salmon and potato fishcakes

The secret of a good fishcake is to make it with freshly prepared fish and potatoes, home-made breadcrumbs and plenty of interesting seasoning. This recipe makes a great mid-week supper, and you can serve the fishcakes with tartare sauce or garlic mayonnaise.

Serves 4

450g/1lb cooked salmon fillet

450g/1lb freshly cooked potatoes, mashed

25g/1oz/2 tbsp butter, melted

10ml/2 tsp wholegrain mustard

15ml/1 tbsp each chopped fresh dill and chopped fresh flat leaf parsley

grated rind and juice of ½ lemon

15g/½oz/1 tbsp plain (all-purpose) flour

1 egg, lightly beaten

150g/5oz/generous 1 cup dried breadcrumbs

60ml/4 tbsp sunflower oil

salt and ground white pepper

rocket (arugula) leaves and fresh chives, to garnish

lemon wedges, to serve

1 Flake the cooked salmon, watching carefully for and discarding any skin and bones. Place the flaked salmon in a bowl with the mashed potato, melted butter and wholegrain mustard. Mix well, then stir in the chopped fresh dill and parsley, lemon rind and juice. Season to taste.

2 Divide the mixture into eight portions and shape each into a ball, then flatten into a thick disc. Dip the fishcakes first in flour, then in egg and finally in breadcrumbs, making sure they are evenly coated.

3 Heat the oil in a frying pan until very hot. Fry the fishcakes in batches until golden brown and crisp all over. As each batch is ready, drain on kitchen paper and keep hot.

4 Warm some plates and place two fishcakes on to each one. Garnish with rocket leaves and chives, and serve with lemon wedges.

Variations
• Almost any fresh white or hot-smoked fish is suitable; smoked cod and haddock are particularly good.
• A mixture of smoked and unsmoked fish also works well, as does a mixture of salmon and chopped prawns (shrimp).

Per portion Energy 586kcal/2453kJ; Protein 29.8g; Carbohydrate 49.9g, of which sugars 3.2g; Fat 31g, of which saturates 7.2g; Cholesterol 117mg; Calcium 79mg; Fibre 1.3g; Sodium 266mg.

Pan-fried trout with citrus and basil

Fillets of freshwater trout or sea trout are pan-fried and served with a fresh, citrus sauce.
This light, summer supper is very good served with new potatoes and samphire.

Serves 4

4 trout fillets, each about 200g/7oz

2 lemons

3 oranges

105ml/7 tbsp olive oil

45ml/3 tbsp plain
(all-purpose) flour

25g/1oz/2 tbsp butter

5ml/1 tsp soft light
brown sugar

15g/½oz/½ cup fresh
basil leaves

salt and ground black pepper

1 Arrange the trout fillets in the base of a non-metallic shallow dish. Grate the rind from one lemon and two of the oranges, then squeeze these fruits and pour the combined juices into a jug (pitcher). Slice the remaining fruits and reserve to use as a garnish.

2 Add 75ml/5 tbsp of the oil to the citrus juices. Beat with a fork and pour over the fish. Cover and leave to marinate in the refrigerator for at least 2 hours.

3 Preheat the oven to 150°C/300°F/ Gas 2. Using a fish slice or metal spatula, carefully remove the trout from the marinade.

4 Season the fish and coat each in flour. Heat the remaining oil in a frying pan and add the fish. Fry for 2–3 minutes on each side until cooked, then transfer to a plate and keep hot in the oven.

5 Add the butter and the marinade to the pan and heat gently, stirring until the butter has melted. Season with salt and pepper, then stir in the sugar. Continue cooking gently for 4–5 minutes until the sauce has thickened slightly.

6 Finely shred half the basil leaves and add them to the pan. Pour the sauce over the fish and garnish with the remaining basil and the orange and lemon slices.

Cook's tip Basil leaves bruise very easily, so they should always be shredded by hand or used whole rather than cut with a knife. Don't use any leaves that are shrivelled or have brown patches on them.

Per portion Energy 266kcal/1119kJ; Protein 40.5g; Carbohydrate 7.9g, of which sugars 7.7g; Fat 8.3g, of which saturates 0.2g; Cholesterol 0mg; Calcium 140mg; Fibre 1.7g; Sodium 177mg.

Fish gratin

Coastal ports are renowned for the quality of their seafood, and this traditional fish dish makes the most of the catch of the day. It is topped with bubbling hot cheese.

Serves 4

400g/14oz firm fish fillets, such as monkfish, salmon, turbot or cod

200g/7oz cooked grey shrimp and/or shelled cooked mussels, or peeled uncooked scampi (extra large shrimp)

1 litre/1¾ pints/4 cups fish stock

100g/3½oz/scant ½ cup butter

50g/2oz/½ cup plain (all-purpose) flour

100ml/3½fl oz/scant ½ cup dry white wine or dry vermouth

100ml/3½fl oz/scant ½ cup double (heavy) cream

115g/4oz/1 cup grated cheese (see Cook's tip)

45ml/3 tbsp chopped fresh parsley

salt and ground white pepper

crusty bread or potato croquettes, to serve

Cook's tip Use a mixture of cheeses. Belgians use a combination of local cheeses, but a mixture of Gruyère and Parmesan cheese also works well. A mixture of cheese and breadcrumbs also makes a good topping.

1 Preheat the oven to 200°C/400°F/ Gas 6. Grease a 1.2 litre/2 pint/5 cup baking dish or four individual dishes.

2 Cut the fish fillets into even cubes, removing any stray bones.

3 Bring the fish stock to the boil in a large pan. Add the fish cubes, reduce the heat and poach for 2 minutes. If using scampi, poach them for 1 minute, until barely pink.

4 As soon as the fish pieces are cooked, lift them out with a slotted spoon and layer in the dish or dishes. Season and cover to keep warm. Pour the fish stock into a measuring jug (cup).

5 Melt the butter in a large pan over a medium heat. When the butter begins to foam, whisk in the flour and stir for 2 minutes.

6 Stirring all the time, add 500ml/ 17fl oz/generous 2 cups of the reserved fish stock in a steady stream, saving the rest to thin the sauce later if necessary. Add the white wine or vermouth in the same way. Simmer for 3 minutes, stirring, then add the cream. Season and simmer for 1 minute more.

7 Remove from the heat and add the grated cheese, reserving 45ml/3 tbsp for the topping. Stir in the grey shrimp and/or mussels, with 15ml/1 tbsp of the parsley, and spoon evenly over the fish. Sprinkle with the reserved cheese.

8 Bake for 10–15 minutes, until the cheese melts and turns golden. Sprinkle with the remaining parsley and serve immediately with crusty bread or potato croquettes.

Per portion Energy 612kcal/2541kJ; Protein 36g; Carbohydrate 10.5g, of which sugars 1g; Fat 45.3g, of which saturates 27.9g; Cholesterol 190mg; Calcium 358mg; Fibre 0.4g; Sodium 531mg.

Whole baked salmon with watercress sauce

Served as an impressive centrepiece, this whole baked salmon would make a stunning focal point for a country dining table. Healthy and delicious, the dish is equally good served hot or cold. The peppery watercress sauce and fresh cucumber complement the salmon perfectly.

Serves 6–8

2–3kg/4½–6½lb salmon, cleaned, with head and tail left on

3–5 spring onions (scallions), thinly sliced

1 lemon, thinly sliced

1 cucumber, thinly sliced

salt and ground black pepper

sprigs of fresh dill, to garnish

lemon wedges, to serve

For the sauce

3 garlic cloves, chopped

200g/7oz watercress leaves, finely chopped

40g/1½oz/¾ cup finely chopped fresh tarragon

300g/11oz/1¼ cups mayonnaise

15–30ml/1–2 tbsp lemon juice

200g/7oz/scant 1 cup unsalted (sweet) butter

1 Preheat the oven to 180°C/350°F/ Gas 4. Rinse the salmon and lay it on a large piece of foil. Stuff the fish with the sliced spring onions and lemon. Season with salt and black pepper.

2 Loosely fold the foil around the fish and fold the edges over to seal. Bake in the preheated oven for about 1 hour.

3 Remove the fish from the oven and leave it to stand, still wrapped in the foil, for about 15 minutes. Then gently unwrap the foil parcel and set the salmon aside to cool.

4 When the fish has cooled, carefully lift it on to a large plate, still covered with lemon slices. Cover the fish tightly with clear film (plastic wrap) and chill for several hours in the refrigerator.

5 Remove the lemon slices from the top of the fish. Use a blunt knife to lift up the edge of the skin and carefully peel the skin away from the flesh, avoiding tearing the flesh. Pull out any fins at the same time. Carefully turn the salmon over and repeat on the other side. Leave the head on for serving, if you wish. Discard the skin.

Variation If you prefer to poach the fish rather than baking it, you will need to use a fish kettle. Place the salmon on the rack in the kettle. Cover the salmon completely with cold water, place the lid over to cover, and slowly bring to a simmer. Cook for 5–10 minutes per 450g/1lb until tender. The fish is cooked when pink and opaque.

6 To make the sauce, put the garlic, watercress, tarragon, mayonnaise and lemon juice in a food processor or bowl, and process or mix to combine.

7 Melt the butter, then add to the watercress mixture a little at a time, processing or stirring until the butter has been incorporated and the sauce is thick and smooth. Cover and chill.

8 Arrange the cucumber slices in overlapping rows along the length of the fish, so that they look like large fish scales. You can also slice the cucumber diagonally to produce longer slices for decoration. Trim the edges with scissors. Serve the fish, garnished with dill and lemon wedges, with the watercress sauce alongside.

Cook's tip Do not prepare the sauce hours before you need it because the watercress will discolour. Alternatively, add the watercress just before serving.

Per portion Energy 1044kcal/4323kJ; Protein 51.6g; Carbohydrate 1.4g, of which sugars 1.2g; Fat 92.4g, of which saturates 28.5g; Cholesterol 231mg; Calcium 135mg; Fibre 0.7g; Sodium 558mg.

Moules marinière

Serve this French country classic with a big bowl of fries and chunks of crusty bread to soak up the sauce. As an alternative, you could try cooking the mussels in Belgian beer.

Serves 2

25g/1oz/2 tbsp butter

300ml/½ pint/1¼ cups dry white wine

1kg/2¼lb mussels, cleaned

45ml/3 tbsp chopped fresh parsley

salt and ground black pepper

Cook's tip Use line-grown mussels if possible and the freshest you can find. Tip them into the sink and rinse several times in cold water before draining well.

1 Heat the butter in a large pan until foaming, then pour in the wine. Bring to the boil.

2 Discard any open mussels that do not close when sharply tapped, and add the remaining ones to the pan.

3 Cover with a tight-fitting lid and cook over a medium heat for 4–5 minutes, shaking the pan every now and then. By this time, all the mussels should have opened. Discard any that are still closed.

4 Line a large sieve (strainer) with kitchen paper and strain the mussels and their liquid through it. Transfer the mussels to warmed serving bowls.

5 Pour the liquid into a small pan and bring to the boil. Season with salt and pepper and stir in the parsley. Pour over the mussels and serve immediately.

Per portion Energy 189kcal/799kJ; Protein 26.4g; Carbohydrate 2.4g, of which sugars 1.9g; Fat 3.1g, of which saturates 0.5g; Cholesterol 60mg; Calcium 308mg; Fibre 0.4g; Sodium 319mg.

Dressed crab with asparagus

Considerably cheaper than lobster, crab meat is just as juicy and flavourful, and at its best when asparagus comes into season. Try this crab dish with a splash of Tabasco sauce.

Serves 4

24 asparagus spears

4 dressed crabs

30ml/2 tbsp mayonnaise

15ml/1 tbsp chopped fresh parsley

1 Wash the asparagus and trim off the bases. Boil in a pan of water for about 7 minutes, until you can spear a stem with the blade of a knife and the blade slips out easily. Plunge the spears into iced water to stop them from cooking further. Drain them when cold, and pat dry with kitchen paper.

2 Scoop out the white crab meat from the shells and claws and place it in a bowl. If you can't find fresh crabs, you can use the same amount of canned or frozen white crab meat. Ensure the meat is completely defrosted and place on to kitchen paper to dry.

3 Add the mayonnaise and chopped fresh parsley and combine with a fork.

4 Place the mixture into the crab shells and add six asparagus spears per serving. Serve with crusty bread and a handful of lightly dressed salad leaves.

Per portion Energy 207kcal/859kJ; Protein 19.5g; Carbohydrate 3g, of which sugars 2.8g; Fat 13g, of which saturates 1.9g; Cholesterol 72mg; Calcium 157mg; Fibre 2.6g; Sodium 540mg.

Seafood pie

A taste of the sea, a good fish pie includes both fresh and smoked fish – ideal winter fare when the fishing fleets are hampered by gales and fresh fish is in short supply. Add shellfish such as mussels, and a few capers and dill for extra piquancy.

Serves 4–5

450g/1lb haddock or cod fillet

225g/8oz smoked haddock or cod

150ml/¼ pint/⅔ cup milk

150ml/¼ pint/⅔ cup water

1 slice of lemon

1 small bay leaf

a few fresh parsley stalks

For the sauce

25g/1oz/2 tbsp butter

25g/1oz/¼ cup plain (all-purpose) flour

5ml/1 tbsp lemon juice, or to taste

45ml/3 tbsp chopped fresh parsley

ground black pepper

For the topping

450g/1lb potatoes, boiled and mashed

25g/1oz/2 tbsp butter

1 Preheat the oven to 190°C/375°F/ Gas 5. Rinse the fish, cut it into manageable pieces and put into a pan with the milk, water, lemon, bay leaf and parsley stalks.

2 Bring the fish slowly to the boil, then simmer gently for 15 minutes until tender. Strain and reserve 300ml/ ½ pint/1¼ cups of the cooking liquor. Leave the fish until cool, then flake the cooked flesh and discard the skin and bones. Set aside.

3 To make the sauce, melt the butter in a heavy pan, add the flour and cook for 1–2 minutes over low heat, stirring constantly.

4 Gradually add the reserved cooking liquor, stirring well to make a smooth sauce.

Variations
• Almost any mixture of prepared seafood can go into this fish pie. Cut all the fish into roughly the same size, and cut large scallops or prawns in half.
• Try adding other soft herbs such as chervil, dill or chives to the sauce, or a teaspoon of grain mustard.

5 Simmer the sauce gently for about 1–2 minutes, then remove the pan from the heat and stir in the flaked fish, chopped parsley and lemon juice. Season to taste with ground black pepper.

6 Turn into a buttered 1.75 litre/3 pint/ 7½ cup pie dish or shallow casserole, cover evenly with the mashed potato for the topping, smoothing with the back of a fork if necessary. Cut the butter into small pieces and dot the potato with the butter.

7 Cook the pie in the preheated oven for about 20 minutes, or until it is thoroughly heated through. The potato topping should be golden brown and crunchy.

8 Divide the pie among four or five warmed plates and serve immediately with a lightly cooked green vegetable, such as fresh broccoli florets.

Per portion Energy 336kcal/1413kJ; Protein 35.1g; Carbohydrate 24.3g, of which sugars 0.9g; Fat 11.6g, of which saturates 6.7g; Cholesterol 87mg; Calcium 45mg; Fibre 1.7g; Sodium 587mg.

Poultry and game

Chicken and other poultry are among the most
popular and versatile meats, and they can be
prepared in a huge variety of ways, from a simple
roasted bird to delicious slow-cooked classics such as
coq au vin. In the past, game was a seasonal meat
available only at certain times of the year, but it is
now possible to obtain a wide variety of game all
year round. It is, however, still rewarding to cook
game with traditional seasonal ingredients.

Roast chicken with herb stuffing

A staple of traditional country cooking, a simply roasted free-range chicken with herbs and home-made stuffing is hard to beat. Serve with roast potatoes, sausages, bacon rolls and seasonal vegetables, along with a fruit jelly such as cranberry sauce or elderberry jelly.

Serves 6

1 large chicken, about 1.8kg/4lb, with giblets and neck if possible

1 small onion, sliced

1 small carrot, sliced

small bunch of parsley and thyme

15g/½oz/1 tbsp butter

30ml/2 tbsp chicken fat or oil

6 rashers (strips) of streaky (fatty) bacon

salt and ground black pepper

For the stuffing

1 onion, finely chopped

50g/2oz/¼ cup butter

150g/5oz/2½ cups fresh white breadcrumbs

15ml/1 tbsp fresh chopped parsley

15ml/1 tbsp fresh chopped mixed herbs, such as thyme, marjoram and chives

finely grated rind and juice of ½ lemon

1 small egg, lightly beaten (optional)

15ml/1 tbsp plain (all-purpose) flour

1 Remove the giblets from the chicken; also remove the piece of fat which is found just inside the vent and put this fat into a roasting pan – it can be rendered down and used when cooking the roast potatoes. Wipe out the inside of the bird thoroughly. Separate the liver from the rest of the giblets, chop it and set it aside to use in the gravy.

2 Put the giblets and the neck into a pan with the sliced onion and sliced carrot, the bunch of parsley and thyme and a good sprinkling of salt and pepper. Add enough cold water to cover generously, bring to the boil and leave to simmer gently for about 1 hour. Strain the chicken stock and discard the giblets. Preheat the oven to 200°C/400°F/Gas 6.

3 Meanwhile, make the herb stuffing: cook the chopped onion in the butter in a large pan over a low heat without colouring for a few minutes until it is just beginning to soften.

4 Remove from the heat, and add the breadcrumbs, fresh herbs and grated lemon rind. Mix thoroughly. Mix in the lemon juice, beaten egg, if using, and salt and pepper. (The egg will bind the stuffing and make it firmer when cooked, but it can be omitted if you prefer a lighter, more crumbly texture.)

5 Spoon the stuffing into the neck cavity of the chicken, without packing it in too tightly, and secure the opening with a small skewer. Spread the breast with the butter, then put the chicken fat or oil into a roasting pan and lay the bird in it. Season and lay the bacon rashers over the top of the bird to protect it in the oven.

6 Weigh the stuffed chicken and work out the cooking time at 20 minutes per 450g/1lb and 20 minutes over, then put into the preheated oven. After 20 minutes, reduce the temperature to 180°C/350°F/Gas 4 for another 45–60 minutes, or until cooked. Test by inserting a sharp knife between the body and thigh: if the juices run clear with no hint of blood, it is cooked.

7 Transfer the cooked chicken to a serving dish and allow it to rest for 10 minutes while you make the gravy.

8 To make the gravy, pour off the excess fat from the roasting pan, then add the finely chopped liver and stir over low heat for 1 minute, or until it has turned light brown. Sprinkle in just enough flour to absorb the remaining chicken fat and cook gently, stirring to blend, for 1 or 2 minutes. Gradually add some of the giblet stock, scraping the pan to dissolve the residues and stirring well to make a smooth gravy.

9 Bring to the boil, stirring, gradually adding more stock until the consistency is as you like it. Adjust the seasoning, and then pour into a heated sauceboat to hand round separately.

10 Carve the chicken. Serve on heated plates with the herb stuffing and gravy.

Per portion Energy 562kcal/2342kJ; Protein 40.9g; Carbohydrate 23.2g, of which sugars 2.7g; Fat 34.5g, of which saturates 11.9g; Cholesterol 216mg; Calcium 72mg; Fibre 1.5g; Sodium 381mg.

Coq au vin

A quintessential French country casserole, this dish is a fricassée made with a cock bird, cooked long and slow in red wine to tenderize the meat. Making it fills the house with appetite-arousing aromas. Serve with boiled potatoes or little fried bread croûtons.

Serves 6

45ml/3 tbsp light olive oil

12 shallots

225g/8oz rindless streaky (fatty) bacon rashers (strips), chopped

3 garlic cloves, finely chopped

225g/8oz small mushrooms, halved

3 boneless chicken breast portions

6 boneless chicken thighs

1 bottle red wine

salt and ground black pepper

45ml/3 tbsp chopped fresh parsley, to garnish

For the bouquet garni

3 sprigs each of fresh parsley, thyme and sage

1 bay leaf

4 peppercorns

For the beurre manié

25g/1oz/2 tbsp butter, softened

25g/1oz/¼ cup plain (all-purpose) flour

Cook's tip Coq au Vin can be made with any full-bodied red wine. A truly authentic recipe would include some of the birds' blood to thicken the sauce, which ends up an almost black sauce.

1 Heat the oil in a large, flameproof casserole, add the shallots and cook for 5 minutes, or until golden. Increase the heat, add the bacon, garlic and halved mushrooms and cook for 10 minutes more, stirring frequently.

2 Use a draining spoon to transfer the cooked ingredients to a plate. Halve the chicken breast portions, then brown, along with the thighs, in the oil remaining in the pan. As they cook, turn them to ensure they are golden brown all over. Return the shallots, garlic, mushrooms and bacon to the casserole and pour in the red wine.

3 Tie the ingredients for the bouquet garni in a bundle in a small piece of muslin (cheesecloth) and add to the casserole. Bring to the boil, reduce the heat and cover the casserole, then simmer for about 35 minutes.

4 To make the beurre manié, cream the butter and flour together in a small bowl using your fingers or a spoon to make a smooth paste.

5 Add small lumps of this paste to the bubbling casserole, stirring well until each piece has melted into the liquid before adding the next. When all the paste has been added, bring back to the boil and simmer for 5 minutes.

6 Season the casserole to taste with salt and pepper and serve garnished with chopped fresh parsley and accompanied by boiled potatoes.

Per portion Energy 496kcal/2067kJ; Protein 39.2g; Carbohydrate 5g, of which sugars 1.8g; Fat 26.9g, of which saturates 8.5g; Cholesterol 153mg; Calcium 47mg; Fibre 1.1g; Sodium 600mg.

Chicken and root vegetable casserole

Tender chunks of starchy root vegetables are the ideal winter comfort food. When cooked slowly in a casserole with chicken, green lentils and creamy mustard sauce, the natural sugars in the vegetables become mellow and intense, giving an irresistible flavour.

Serves 4

350g/12oz onions

350g/12oz leeks

225g/8oz carrots

450g/1lb swede (rutabaga)

30ml/2 tbsp oil

4 chicken portions, about 900g/2lb total weight

115g/4oz/$\frac{1}{2}$ cup green lentils

475ml/16fl oz/2 cups chicken stock

300ml/$\frac{1}{2}$ pint/1$\frac{1}{4}$ cups apple juice

10ml/2 tsp cornflour (cornstarch)

45ml/3 tbsp crème fraîche

10ml/2 tsp wholegrain mustard

30ml/2 tbsp chopped fresh tarragon

salt and ground black pepper

fresh tarragon sprigs, to garnish

3 Add the onions to the casserole and cook for 5 minutes, stirring, until they begin to soften and colour. Add the leeks, carrots, swede and lentils to the casserole and stir over a medium heat for 2 minutes.

4 Return the chicken to the pan, then add the stock, apple juice and seasoning. Bring to the boil and cover. Reduce the heat and cook for 50–60 minutes, or until the chicken and lentils are tender.

5 In a small bowl, blend the cornflour with about 30ml/2 tbsp water to make a smooth paste and then add to the casserole with the crème fraîche, wholegrain mustard and chopped tarragon.

6 Adjust the seasoning to taste, then simmer the casserole gently for about 2 minutes, stirring constantly, until thickened slightly. Garnish with the tarragon sprigs, and then serve in individual bowls.

1 Prepare the onions, leeks, carrots and swede and roughly chop them into even pieces.

2 Heat the oil in a large flameproof casserole. Season the chicken portions with plenty of salt and pepper and brown them in the hot oil until golden. Drain on kitchen paper.

Per portion Energy 477kcal/2010kJ; Protein 46.8g; Carbohydrate 45.7g, of which sugars 24.9g; Fat 13.2g, of which saturates 4.5g; Cholesterol 118mg; Calcium 151mg; Fibre 8.1g; Sodium 141mg.

Creamy chicken and mushroom pie

A family favourite, this classic pie includes porcini mushrooms, which give an intense mushroom flavour, topped with a melt-in-the-mouth pastry crust.

Serves 6

15g/½oz/¼ cup dried porcini mushrooms

50g/2oz/¼ cup butter

30ml/2 tbsp plain (all-purpose) flour

250ml/8fl oz/1 cup hot chicken stock

60ml/4 tbsp single (light) cream

1 onion, coarsely chopped

2 carrots, sliced

2 celery sticks, coarsely chopped

50g/2oz/¾ cup fresh mushrooms, quartered

450g/1lb cooked chicken meat, cubed

50g/2oz/½ cup fresh or frozen peas

salt and ground black pepper

beaten egg, to glaze

For the pastry

225g/8oz/2 cups plain (all-purpose) flour

1.5ml/¼ tsp salt

115g/4oz/½ cup cold butter, diced

65g/2½oz/⅓ cup white vegetable fat, diced

60–120ml/4–8 tbsp chilled water

1 To make the pastry, sift the flour and salt into a bowl. Cut or rub in the butter and white vegetable fat until the mixture resembles fine breadcrumbs. Sprinkle with 90ml/ 6 tbsp chilled water and mix until the dough holds together. If the dough is too crumbly, add a little more water, 15ml/1 tbsp at a time.

2 Gather the dough into a ball and flatten it into a round. Wrap and chill for at least 30 minutes.

3 To make the filling, put the mushrooms in a bowl. Cover with hot water and soak for 30 minutes. Drain in a muslin- (cheesecloth-) lined sieve (strainer), then dry on kitchen paper. Preheat the oven to 190°C/375°F/Gas 5.

4 Melt half of the butter in a heavy pan. Whisk in the flour and cook until bubbling, whisking constantly. Add the hot stock and whisk over a medium heat until the mixture boils. Cook for 2–3 minutes, then whisk in the cream. Season to taste, and set aside.

5 Heat the remaining butter in a non-stick frying pan and cook the onion and carrots over a low heat for 5 minutes. Add the celery and fresh mushrooms and cook for 5 minutes more. Stir in the cooked chicken, peas and drained porcini mushrooms.

6 Add the chicken mixture to the hot cream sauce and stir to mix. Adjust the seasoning if necessary. Spoon the mixture into a 2.5 litre/4 pint/2½ quart oval baking dish.

7 Roll out the pastry to a thickness of about 3mm/⅛in. Cut out an oval 2.5cm/1in larger all around than the dish. Lay the pastry over the filling. Gently press around the edge of the dish to seal, then trim off the excess pastry. Crimp the edge of the pastry by pushing the forefinger of one hand into the edge and, using the thumb and forefinger of the other hand, pinch the pastry. Continue all round the pastry edge.

8 Press together the pastry trimmings and roll out again. Cut out mushroom shapes with a knife and stick them on to the pastry lid with beaten egg. Glaze the lid with egg and cut several slits in the pastry to allow the steam to escape. Bake the pie for about 30 minutes, until the pastry has browned. Serve hot.

Per portion Energy 576kcal/2403kJ; Protein 23.8g; Carbohydrate 39.6g, of which sugars 4.7g; Fat 36.9g, of which saturates 20.3g; Cholesterol 127mg; Calcium 104mg; Fibre 3.1g; Sodium 334mg.

Classic roast turkey with country stuffing

Traditionally served at Christmas or Thanksgiving, roast turkey is a splendid celebration dish. The rich herb stuffing in this recipe is made with calf's liver, but lamb's liver would be fine, too. Serve with cranberry jelly, which will taste even better if you make it yourself.

Serves 6

1 turkey, about 4.5–5.5kg/10–12lb, washed and patted dry with kitchen paper

25g/1oz/2 tbsp butter, melted

salt and ground black pepper, to taste

cranberry jelly, to serve

For the stuffing

200g/7oz/3½ cups fresh white breadcrumbs

175ml/6fl oz/¾ cup milk

25g/1oz/2 tbsp butter

1 egg, separated

1 calf's liver, about 600g/1lb 6oz, finely chopped

2 onions, finely chopped

90ml/6 tbsp chopped fresh dill

10ml/2 tsp clear honey

salt and ground black pepper, to taste

1 To make the stuffing, put the breadcrumbs and milk in a large bowl and soak until swollen and soft.

2 Melt the butter in a frying pan and mix 5ml/1 tsp with the egg yolk.

3 Heat the remaining butter in a frying pan and add the finely chopped calf's liver and onions. Fry gently for 5 minutes, until the onions are golden brown. Remove from the heat and leave to cool.

4 Preheat the oven to 180°C/350°F/ Gas 4. Add the cooled liver mixture to the soaked breadcrumbs and milk, then add the butter and egg yolk mixture, with the chopped dill, clear honey and seasoning.

5 In a clean bowl, whisk the egg white to soft peaks, then fold into the stuffing mixture, stirring gently to combine thoroughly.

6 Season the turkey inside and out with salt and pepper. Stuff the cavity with the stuffing mixture, then weigh to calculate the cooking time. Allow 20 minutes per 500g/1¼lb, plus an additional 20 minutes. Tuck the legs of the turkey inside the cavity and tie the end shut with string. Brush the outside with melted butter and transfer to a roasting pan. Place in the oven and roast for the calculated time.

7 Baste the turkey regularly during cooking, and cover with foil for the final 30 minutes if the skin becomes too brown. To test whether the turkey is cooked, pierce the thickest part of the thigh with a knife; the juices should run clear.

8 Remove the turkey from the oven, cover with foil and leave to rest for about 15 minutes. Carve into thin slices, then spoon over the juices and serve with the stuffing and cranberry jelly.

Per portion Energy 740kcal/3126kJ; Protein 112.3g; Carbohydrate 35.9g, of which sugars 7.3g; Fat 13.5g, of which saturates 6.6g; Cholesterol 507mg; Calcium 122mg; Fibre 1.7g; Sodium 517mg.

Roast pheasant with sherry mustard sauce

It is best to use only young pheasants for roasting – older birds are too tough and are only suitable for casseroles. Serve this succulent dish with potatoes braised in wine with garlic and onions, bread sauce and winter vegetables such as Brussels sprouts or red cabbage.

Serves 4

2 young oven-ready pheasants

50g/2oz/¼ cup softened butter

200ml/7fl oz/scant 1 cup sherry

15ml/1 tbsp Dijon mustard

salt and ground black pepper

Cook's tip To keep the meat moist, add bacon rashers (strips) to the pheasants before putting them in the oven. Remove 20 minutes before the end of cooking.

1 Preheat the oven to 200°C/400°F/ Gas 6. Put the pheasants in a roasting pan and spread the butter all over both birds. Season with salt and pepper.

2 Roast the pheasants for 50 minutes, basting often to stop the birds from drying out. When the pheasants are cooked, take them out of the pan and leave to rest on a board, covered with foil.

3 Meanwhile, place the roasting pan over a medium heat. Add the sherry and season with salt and pepper. Simmer for 5 minutes, until the sherry has slightly reduced, then stir in the mustard. Carve the pheasants and serve with the sherry and mustard sauce.

Per portion Energy 692kcal/2897kJ; Protein 81.7g; Carbohydrate 1.2g, of which sugars 1.1g; Fat 34.2g, of which saturates 14.5g; Cholesterol 27mg; Calcium 133mg; Fibre 0g; Sodium 456mg.

Roast farmyard duck with apples and cider

The combination of the apples and cider in this recipe makes a fine sauce which complements the rich meat of roast duck or goose perfectly. Serve with a selection of vegetables, including roast potatoes and, perhaps, some red cabbage.

Serves 4

2kg/4½lb oven-ready duck
or duckling

300ml/½ pint/1¼ cups dry
(hard) cider

60ml/4 tbsp double (heavy) cream

sea salt and ground black pepper

For the stuffing

75g/3oz/6 tbsp butter

115g/4oz/2 cups fresh
white breadcrumbs

450g/1lb cooking apples,
peeled, cored and diced

15ml/1 tbsp sugar, or to taste

freshly grated nutmeg

1 Preheat the oven to 200°C/400°F/ Gas 6. To make the stuffing, melt the butter in a pan and fry the breadcrumbs until golden brown. Add the apples to the breadcrumbs with salt, pepper, the sugar and a pinch of nutmeg. Mix well.

2 Wipe the duck out with a clean, damp cloth, and remove any obvious excess fat (including the flaps just inside the vent). Rub the skin with salt. Stuff the duck with the prepared mixture, then secure the vent with a small skewer.

3 Weigh the stuffed duck and calculate the cooking time, allowing 20 minutes per 450g/1lb. Prick the skin all over with a fork to allow the fat to run out during the cooking time, then lay it on top of a wire rack in a roasting pan, sprinkle with freshly ground black pepper and put it into the preheated oven to roast.

4 About 20 minutes before the end of the estimated cooking time, remove the duck from the oven and pour off all the fat that has accumulated under the rack (reserve it for frying). Slide the duck off the rack into the roasting pan and pour the cider over it. Return to the oven and finish cooking, basting occasionally.

5 When the duck is cooked, remove it from the pan and keep warm while you make the sauce. Set the roasting pan over a medium heat and boil the cider to reduce it by half. Stir in the cream, heat through and season. Meanwhile, remove the stuffing from the duck. Carve the duck into slices or quarter it using poultry shears. Serve with a portion of stuffing and the cider sauce.

Per portion Energy 572kcal/2397kJ; Protein 31.5g; Carbohydrate 34.6g, of which sugars 13.1g; Fat 33.1g, of which saturates 17.8g; Cholesterol 211mg; Calcium 74mg; Fibre 2.4g; Sodium 498mg.

Game pie

This impressive country pie can be made with whichever game birds are available. Add in some freshly foraged mushrooms and serve the pie with puréed Jerusalem artichokes and winter greens such as purple sprouting broccoli or Brussels sprouts.

Serves 8–10

2 game birds, such as skinless pheasant and/or pigeon

225g/8oz lean stewing steak

115g/4oz streaky (fatty) bacon, trimmed

butter, for frying

2 medium onions, finely chopped

1 large garlic clove, crushed

15ml/1 tbsp plain (all-purpose) flour

about 300ml/½ pint/¼ cup pigeon or pheasant stock

15ml/1 tbsp tomato purée (paste) (optional)

15ml/1 tbsp chopped fresh parsley

a little grated lemon rind

15ml/1 tbsp rowan or redcurrant jelly

50–115g/2–4oz button (white) mushrooms, halved or quartered if large

a small pinch of freshly grated nutmeg or ground cloves (optional)

milk or beaten egg, to glaze

sea salt and ground black pepper

For the rough-puff pastry

225g/8oz/2 cups plain (all-purpose) flour

2.5ml/½ tsp salt

5ml/1 tsp lemon juice

115g/4oz/½ cup butter, in walnut-sized pieces

1 To make the rough-puff pastry, sieve (sift) the flour and salt into a large mixing bowl. Add the lemon juice and the butter pieces and just enough cold water to bind the ingredients together. Turn the mixture on to a floured board and roll the pastry into a long strip. Fold it into three and press the edges together. Half-turn the pastry, rib it with the rolling pin to equalize the air in it and roll it into a strip once again. Repeat this folding and rolling process three more times.

2 Slice the pheasant or pigeon breasts from the bone and cut the meat into fairly thin strips. Trim away any fat from the stewing steak and slice it in the same manner. Cut the streaky bacon into thin strips, and then cook it very gently in a heavy frying pan until the fat runs. Add some butter and brown the sliced pigeon or pheasant and stewing steak in it, a little at a time.

3 Remove the meats from the pan and set aside. Cook the onions and garlic in the fat for 2–3 minutes over a medium heat. Remove and set aside with the meats, then stir the flour into the remaining fat. Cook for 1–2 minutes, and then gradually stir in enough stock to make a fairly thin gravy. Add the tomato purée, if using, parsley, lemon rind and rowan or redcurrant jelly and the mushrooms. Season to taste and add the nutmeg or cloves, if you like.

4 Return the browned meats, chopped onion and garlic to the pan containing the gravy, and mix well before turning into a deep 1.75 litre/3 pint/7½ cup pie dish. Leave to cool. Meanwhile, preheat the oven to 220°C/425°F/Gas 7.

5 Roll the prepared pastry out to make a circle 2.5cm/1in larger all round than the pie dish, and cut out to make a lid for the pie. Wet the rim of the pie dish and line with the remaining pastry strip. Dampen the strip and cover with the lid, pressing down well to seal.

6 Trim away any excess pastry and knock up the edges with a knife. Make a hole in the centre for the steam to escape and use any pastry trimmings to decorate the top. Glaze the top of the pie with milk or beaten egg. Bake in the oven for about 20 minutes, until the pastry is well-risen, then reduce the oven to 150°C/300°F/Gas 2 for another 1½ hours, until cooked. Protect the pastry from over-browning if necessary by covering it with a double layer of wet baking parchment. Serve.

Cook's tip Frozen puff pastry could replace the home-made rough-puff pastry, if you prefer.

Per portion Energy 448kcal/1871kJ; Protein 28.3g; Carbohydrate 29.5g, of which sugars 5.3g; Fat 24.9g, of which saturates 9.5g; Cholesterol 55mg; Calcium 67mg; Fibre 1.5g; Sodium 393mg.

Venison pie with root vegetable mash

A variation on cottage pie, this tasty game pie has tender pieces of venison cooked in a rich gravy. It makes an excellent winter supper dish, served with steamed green vegetables.

Serves 6

30ml/2 tbsp olive oil

2 leeks, trimmed and chopped

1kg/2¼lb minced (ground) venison

30ml/2 tbsp chopped
fresh parsley

300ml/½ pint/1¼ cups game
consommé

salt and ground black pepper

For the topping

1.5kg/3¼lb mixed root vegetables,
such as sweet potatoes, parsnips and
swede (rutabaga), coarsely chopped

15ml/1 tbsp horseradish sauce

25g/1oz/2 tbsp butter

1 Heat the oil in a pan. Add the leeks and cook for about 8 minutes, or until softened and beginning to brown.

2 Add the minced venison to the pan and cook for about 10 minutes, stirring frequently, or until the meat is well browned. Stir in the chopped parsley, consommé and seasoning, then bring to the boil, cover and simmer for about 20 minutes, stirring occasionally.

3 Meanwhile, preheat the oven to 200°C/400°F/Gas 6 and prepare the topping. Cook the vegetables in boiling, salted water to cover for 15–20 minutes. Drain and mash with the horseradish sauce, butter and pepper.

4 Spoon the venison mixture into an ovenproof dish and top with the mashed vegetables. Bake for 20 minutes, or until piping hot and beginning to brown.

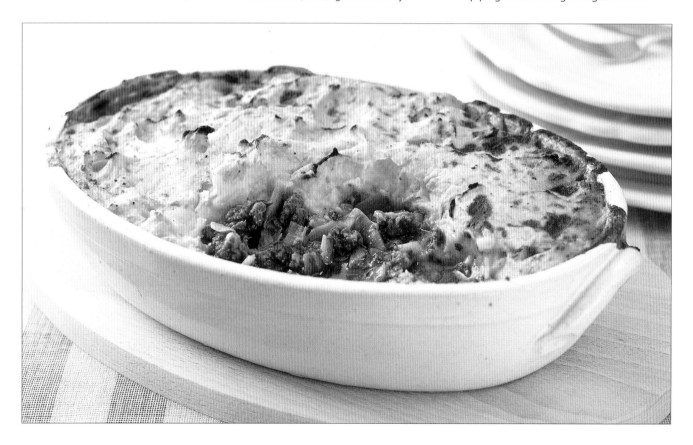

Per portion Energy 307kcal/1291kJ; Protein 39.8g; Carbohydrate 13.2g, of which sugars 12.5g; Fat 12g, of which saturates 4.1g; Cholesterol 93mg; Calcium 154mg; Fibre 5.8g; Sodium 176mg.

Slow-braised rabbit

Long, slow cooking is the secret to the tender rabbit in this dish. It is delicious served with potatoes boiled in their skins and lightly cooked green vegetables such as leeks.

Serves 4–6

1 rabbit, prepared and jointed by the butcher

30ml/2 tbsp seasoned flour

30ml/2 tbsp olive oil or vegetable oil

25g/1oz/2 tbsp butter

115g/4oz streaky (fatty) bacon

1 onion, roughly chopped

2 or 3 carrots, sliced

1 or 2 celery sticks, trimmed and sliced

300ml/½ pint/1¼ cups chicken stock

300ml/½ pint/1¼ cups dry (hard) cider or stout

a small bunch of parsley leaves, chopped

salt and ground black pepper

1 Soak the joints in cold salted water for at least 2 hours, then pat them dry with kitchen paper and toss them in seasoned flour. Preheat the oven to 200°C/400°F/Gas 6.

2 Heat the oil and butter together in a heavy flameproof casserole. Shake off (and reserve) any excess flour from the rabbit joints and brown them on all sides. Lift out and set aside.

3 Add the bacon to the casserole and cook for a few minutes, then remove and set aside with the rabbit.

4 Add the vegetables to the casserole and cook gently until just colouring, then sprinkle over any remaining seasoned flour to absorb the fats in the casserole. Stir over a low heat for 1 minute, to cook the flour. Add the stock and cider or stout, stirring, to make a smooth sauce.

5 Return the rabbit and bacon to the casserole, and add half of the chopped parsley and a light seasoning of salt and pepper. Mix gently together, then cover with a lid and put into the preheated oven. Cook for 15 20 minutes, then reduce the temperature to 150°C/300°F/Gas 2 for about 1½ hours, or until the rabbit is tender. Add the remaining parsley and serve.

Per portion Energy 368kcal/1535kJ; Protein 32.9g; Carbohydrate 10.5g, of which sugars 5.8g; Fat 19.7g, of which saturates 8g; Cholesterol 133mg; Calcium 88mg; Fibre 1.4g; Sodium 567mg.

Meat dishes

Freshly baked pies, slow-cooked pot roasts and
flavoursome casseroles sum up all that is best in
country cooking. From simple Sunday roasts to
comfort food such as shepherd's pie and meat loaf,
there is a meat dish for every occasion in this
chapter. Many of the recipes use economic cuts
of meat and seasonal vegetables, so you can really
make the most of the revival in home cooking.

Roast loin of pork with apple and spinach

Pork and apple are a well-loved combination, and loin of pork is a prime roasting joint. In this recipe the pork is stuffed with apples, but these could be replaced with apricots or prunes.

Serves 6–8

1.6–1.8kg/3½–4lb loin of pork, boned and skinned

1 onion, sliced

juice of 1 orange

15ml/1 tbsp wholegrain mustard

30ml/2 tbsp demerara (raw) sugar

salt and ground black pepper

For the stuffing

50g/2oz spinach

50g/2oz/¼ cup dried apricots, chopped

50g/2oz Cheddar cheese, grated

1 cooking apple, peeled and grated

grated rind of ½ orange

1 Blanch the spinach in boiling water, chop, and put in a bowl with the other stuffing ingredients. Mix well together. Preheat the oven to 180°C/350°F/Gas 4.

2 Place the loin of pork, fat side down, on a board and place the stuffing down the centre. Roll the meat up and tie with cotton string. Season and put it into a roasting pan with the onion and 60ml/4 tbsp water. Cook uncovered for about 35 minutes per 450g/1lb.

3 About 40 minutes before the end of the estimated cooking time, pour off the cooking liquid into a small pan and discard the onion. Add the orange juice to the cooking liquid.

4 Spread the joint with mustard and sprinkle with the sugar. Return it to the oven and increase to 200°C/400°F/Gas 6 for 15 minutes or until crisp.

5 Meanwhile, boil up the juices and reduce to make a thin sauce. Serve with the sliced meat.

Per portion Energy 330kcal/1385kJ; Protein 49.4g; Carbohydrate 6.9g, of which sugars 6.3g; Fat 11.6g, of which saturates 4.9g; Cholesterol 145mg; Calcium 105mg; Fibre 1.2g; Sodium 227mg.

Roast pork belly with caramelized vegetables

Topped with crackling, this melting pork is served with root vegetables. The layer of fat keeps the meat moist. To ensure crisp crackling, make sure the skin is dry before roasting.

Serves 4–6

1 small swede (rutabaga), weighing about 500g/1lb 2oz

1 onion

1 parsnip

2 carrots

15ml/1 tbsp olive oil

1.5kg/3lb 6oz belly of pork, well scored

15ml/1 tbsp fresh thyme leaves or 5ml/1 tsp dried thyme

sea salt flakes and ground black pepper

Cook's tip Ask your butcher to score (slash) the pork rind really well, or use a strong sharp blade and (with care) do it yourself.

1 Preheat the oven to 220°C/425°F/ Gas 7. Cut the vegetables into small cubes (about 2cm/³⁄₄in) and stir them with the oil in a roasting pan, tossing them until evenly coated. Pour in 300ml/½ pint/1¼ cups water.

2 Sprinkle the pork rind with thyme, salt and pepper, rubbing them well into the scored slashes in the pork belly. Place the pork on top of the vegetables, pressing it down so that it sits level, with the skin side uppermost.

3 Put the pork and vegetables into the hot oven and cook for about 30 minutes, by which time the liquid will have almost evaporated to leave a nice golden crust in the bottom of the pan. Remove the pan from the oven.

4 Add 600ml/1 pint/2½ cups cold water to the vegetables in the pan. Reduce the oven temperature to 180°C/350°F/Gas 4.

5 Cook for 1½ hours, or until the pork is tender and the juices run clear when the centre of the meat is pierced with a sharp knife. Check the oven during the final 30 minutes to make sure the liquid does not dry up, adding a little water if necessary.

6 If the crackling is not yet crisp enough, increase the oven temperature to 220°C/425°F/Gas 7 and continue cooking for another 10–20 minutes, adding extra water if necessary – just enough to prevent the vegetables from burning on the bottom of the pan.

7 With a sharp knife, slice off the crackling. Serve it with thick slices of the pork, some vegetables and the golden juices spooned over.

Per portion Energy 1014kcal/4194kJ; Protein 39.5g; Carbohydrate 9.4g, of which sugars 7.3g; Fat 91.2g, of which saturates 33.1g; Cholesterol 180mg; Calcium 81mg; Fibre 3.3g; Sodium 202mg.

Cider-glazed ham

Succulent, moist and with plenty of flavour, this old-fashioned English country recipe keeps the meat tender with a lovely sticky glaze, which is complemented by the fruit and port sauce. It is perfect to share with friends and family at Christmas or any time of the year.

Serves 8–10

2kg/4½lb middle gammon (cured ham) joint

1 large or 2 small onions

about 30 whole cloves

3 bay leaves

10 black peppercorns

1.3 litres/2½ pints/5⅔ cups medium-dry (hard) cider

45ml/3 tbsp soft light brown sugar

bunch of flat leaf parsley, to garnish

For the cranberry sauce

350g/12oz/3 cups cranberries

175g/6oz/¾ cup soft light brown sugar

grated rind and juice of 2 clementines

30ml/2 tbsp port

1 Weigh the gammon and calculate the cooking time at 20 minutes per 450g/1lb, then place it in a large flameproof casserole or pan. Stud the onion or onions with 5–10 of the cloves and add to the casserole or pan with the bay leaves and peppercorns. Add 1.2 litres/2 pints/5 cups of the cider and enough water just to cover the gammon.

2 Heat until simmering and then carefully skim off the scum that rises to the surface using a large spoon or ladle. Start timing the cooking from the moment the stock begins to simmer.

3 Cover the gammon with a lid or foil and simmer gently for the calculated time. Towards the end of the cooking time, preheat the oven to 220°C/425°F/Gas 7.

4 Heat the sugar and remaining cider in a pan; stir until the sugar has dissolved. Simmer for 5 minutes to make a dark, sticky glaze. Remove the pan from the heat and leave to cool for 5 minutes.

Cook's tips
• Leave the gammon until it is just cool enough to handle before removing the rind. Snip off the string using a sharp knife or scissors, then carefully slice off the rind, leaving a thin, even layer of fat. Use a narrow-bladed, sharp knife for the best results.
• A large stockpot is ideal for cooking a big piece of meat like this gammon, but a deep roasting pan will do in an emergency, with foil as a cover and turning the meat often for even cooking.

5 Lift the gammon out of the pan. Carefully and evenly, cut the rind from the meat, then score the fat into a diamond pattern. Place the gammon in a large roasting pan or ovenproof dish.

6 Press a clove into the centre of each diamond, then carefully spoon over the glaze. Bake for 20–25 minutes, or until the fat is brown, glistening and crisp.

7 To make the sauce, simmer all the ingredients in a pan for 20 minutes, stirring. Transfer to a jug (pitcher). Serve the gammon hot or cold, garnished with parsley and the cranberry sauce.

Per portion Energy 447kcal/1873kJ; Protein 44.1g; Carbohydrate 25.6g, of which sugars 25.6g; Fat 18.8g, of which saturates 6.3g; Cholesterol 58mg; Calcium 35mg; Fibre 1.3g; Sodium 2203mg.

Toad-in-the-hole

Resembling toads peeping out of holes, this country favourite can be made with any variety of sausage. Try venison or wild boar, and replace the chives with shredded fresh sage leaves.

Serves 4–6

175g/6oz/1½ cups plain (all-purpose) flour

30ml/2 tbsp chopped fresh chives (optional)

2 eggs

300ml/½ pint/1¼ cups milk

50g/2oz/¼ cup white vegetable fat or lard

450g/1lb good-quality pork sausages

salt and ground black pepper

Cook's tip To ensure really light and crisp batter, ensure that the pan is very hot before adding the batter.

1 Preheat the oven to 220°C/425°F/ Gas 7. Sift the flour into a bowl with a pinch of salt and pepper. Make a well in the centre of the flour. Whisk the chives, if using, with the eggs and milk, then pour this into the well in the flour. Gradually whisk the flour into the liquid to make a smooth batter. Cover and leave to stand for at least 30 minutes.

2 Put the fat into a small roasting pan and place in the oven for 3–5 minutes. Add the pork sausages and cook for 15 minutes. Turn the sausages twice during cooking.

3 Pour the batter over the sausages and return to the oven. Cook for about 20 minutes, or until the batter is risen and golden. Serve immediately.

Per portion Energy 497kcal/2070kJ; Protein 14.5g; Carbohydrate 32.1g, of which sugars 3.8g; Fat 35.4g, of which saturates 13.6g; Cholesterol 109mg; Calcium 141mg; Fibre 1.3g; Sodium 616mg.

Bacon, egg and leek pie

The mild onion flavour of leeks is lovely with the bacon and eggs. The creamy filling is topped with flaky puff pastry, but shortcrust pastry would also work well.

Serves 4–6

15ml/1 tbsp olive oil

200g/7oz lean back bacon rashers (strips), trimmed of rinds and cut into thin strips

250g/9oz/2 cups leeks, thinly sliced

40g/1½oz/⅓ cup plain (all-purpose) flour

1.5ml/¼ tsp freshly grated nutmeg

450ml/¾ pint/scant 2 cups milk, plus extra for brushing

4 eggs

1 sheet ready-rolled puff pastry

salt and ground black pepper

1 Preheat the oven to 200°C/400°F/ Gas 6. Put the oil and bacon in a pan and cook for 5 minutes, stirring occasionally, until the bacon is golden brown. Add the leeks. Stir, cover and cook over medium heat for 5 minutes until softened, stirring once or twice. Stir in the flour and nutmeg. Remove from the heat and gradually stir in the milk.

2 Return to the heat and cook, stirring, until the sauce thickens and boils. Season, then pour into a shallow ovenproof pie dish, measuring 25cm/ 10in in diameter. Make four wells in the sauce and break an egg into each one.

3 Brush the edges of the dish with milk. Lay the pastry over the dish. Trim off the excess pastry and use it to make the trimmings. Brush the backs with milk and stick them on the top of the pie.

4 Brush the pastry with milk and make a small central slit to allow steam to escape. Put into the oven and cook for about 40 minutes until the pastry is puffed up and golden brown, and the eggs have set.

Per portion Energy 202kcal/842kJ; Protein 13.4g; Carbohydrate 9.7g, of which sugars 4.4g; Fat 12.5g, of which saturates 4.2g; Cholesterol 149mg; Calcium 125mg; Fibre 1.1g; Sodium 592mg.

Lamb with honey, rosemary and cider

Country lamb with honey and rosemary are traditional partners. Here, they are teamed with cider and cooked until the meat is meltingly soft and the sweet juices are deliciously caramelized and golden. Slow-cooking this economic cut of lamb ensures that the finished dish is beautifully tender, and the addition of cider gives a lovely tangy flavour. Serve with some golden roast potatoes and green vegetables, such as spinach leaves or beans.

Serves 4–6

1.5kg/3lb 6oz shoulder of lamb

2 garlic cloves, halved

fresh rosemary sprigs

75ml/5 tbsp clear honey

300ml/½ pint/1¼ cups dry (hard) cider, plus extra if necessary

lemon juice (optional)

salt and ground black pepper

1 Preheat the oven to 220°C/425°F/Gas 7. Rub the lamb with the cut garlic. Put the meat and the garlic in a deep roasting pan. Season with salt and pepper.

2 Make small slashes in the meat with a knife and push in a few small sprigs of rosemary.

3 Stir the honey into the cider until it has fully dissolved and then pour it over the lamb.

4 Put the roasting pan into the hot oven and cook the lamb for 20–30 minutes until it has browned and the juices have reduced, begun to caramelize and turn golden brown. Keep checking to make sure the liquid does not dry up and brown too much. If so, add a little water.

5 Stir 300ml/½ pint water into the pan juices and spoon them over the lamb. Cover with a large tent of foil, scrunching the edges around the rim of the pan to seal them.

6 Put the pan back into the oven, reduce the temperature to 180°C/350°F/Gas 4 and cook for about another hour.

7 Remove the foil and spoon the juices over the lamb again. Turn the oven temperature back up to 220°C/425°F/Gas 7 and continue cooking, uncovered, for a further 10–15 minutes, until the lamb is crisp and brown.

8 Lift the lamb on to a serving plate and leave in a warm place to rest for 15 minutes before carving.

9 While the lamb is resting, spoon any excess fat off the top of the juices in the pan. Then taste the juices and adjust the seasoning, if necessary, adding lemon juice to taste. Put the roasting pan on the hob and bring just to the boil.

10 Serve the carved lamb with the juices spooned over.

Cook's tip Though it looks attractive when the rosemary stands proud of the lamb, it is likely to burn. So make sure the slashes are deep and that you push the rosemary sprigs into the lamb.

Variation Medium dry white wine, apple juice, light vegetable stock or water could be used in place of cider.

Per portion Energy 524kcal/2180kJ; Protein 35.3g; Carbohydrate 10.9g, of which sugars 10.9g; Fat 36.5g, of which saturates 17g; Cholesterol 153mg; Calcium 17mg; Fibre 0g; Sodium 130mg.

Country hotpot

Authentically made with mutton and lamb's kidney, this dish is now more often made with neck of lamb and vegetables, including turnips, carrots and leeks and potato.

Serves 4

40g/1½oz/3 tbsp dripping, or 45ml/3 tbsp oil

8 middle neck lamb chops, about 1kg/2¼lb total weight

175g/6oz lamb's kidneys, cut into large pieces

1kg/2¼lb potatoes, thinly sliced

3 carrots, thickly sliced

450g/1lb leeks, sliced

3 celery sticks, sliced

15ml/1 tbsp chopped fresh thyme

30ml/2 tbsp chopped fresh parsley

small sprig of rosemary

600ml/1 pint/2½ cups veal stock

salt and ground black pepper

Variations
• Pork chops can be used instead of lamb. Use thick loin chops or boneless sparerib chops, as preferred.
• Try adding the shredded leaves from a couple of sprigs of sage instead of the rosemary.

1 Preheat the oven to 170°C/325°F/ Gas 3. Heat the dripping or oil in a frying pan and brown the lamb chops and lamb's kidneys in batches, then reserve the fat.

2 In a large casserole, make alternate layers of lamb chops, kidneys, three-quarters of the potatoes and the carrots, leeks and celery, sprinkling the herbs and seasoning over each layer as you go. Tuck the rosemary sprig down the side.

3 Arrange the remaining potatoes on top. Pour over the stock, brush with the reserved fat, then cover and bake for 2½ hours. Increase the oven temperature to 220°C/425°F/Gas 7. Uncover and cook for 30 minutes until well browned on top.

Per portion Energy 724kcal/3035kJ; Protein 51.6g; Carbohydrate 50g, of which sugars 8.7g; Fat 36.7g, of which saturates 13.6g; Cholesterol 278mg; Calcium 75mg; Fibre 7.3g; Sodium 233mg.

Shepherd's pie

A thrifty way to use up leftover roast lamb, this is one of the best-known country dishes.
It can also be made with beef instead of lamb, in which case it is known as cottage pie.

Serves 4

1kg/2½lb potatoes, peeled

60ml/4 tbsp milk

about 25g/1oz/2 tbsp butter

15ml/1 tbsp oil

1 large onion, finely chopped

1 medium carrot, finely chopped

450g/1lb cold cooked lamb,
minced (ground)

150ml/½ pint/⅔ cup lamb stock

30ml/2 tbsp finely chopped
fresh parsley

salt and ground black pepper

Variations
• To make a cottage pie, replace
the lamb and lamb stock with beef.
• Add extra ingredients to the meat
base, such as chopped garlic, a few
mushrooms, a spoonful of tomato
purée (paste) or ketchup, or a splash
of Worcestershire sauce.
• Mix the potatoes with mashed
parsnip, squash or swede (rutabaga),
and a dollop of wholegrain mustard.

1 Preheat the oven to 190°C/375°F/
Gas 5. Boil the potatoes in salted water
for about 20 minutes or until soft.
Drain, and mash with the milk, adding
butter and seasoning to taste.

2 Heat the oil in a frying pan and
add the onion and carrot. Cook over
medium heat for 5–10 minutes, stirring
occasionally, until soft. Stir in the
minced lamb, stock and parsley.

3 Spread the meat mixture in an
ovenproof dish and spoon the mashed
potato evenly over the top. Cook in the
hot oven for about 30 minutes until
the potatoes are crisped and browned.

Per portion Energy 487kcal/2045kJ; Protein 29.4g; Carbohydrate 50.1g, of which sugars 15.2g; Fat 20.2g, of which saturates 8.4g; Cholesterol 69mg; Calcium 54mg; Fibre 5.3g; Sodium 379mg.

Rib of beef with Yorkshire puddings

A quintessential Sunday-lunch classic, this is the well-loved 'roast beef of old England', traditionally served with crisp Yorkshire puddings, golden roast potatoes and a selection of seasonal green and root vegetables, all covered in mouth-watering gravy and accompanied by a tangy horseradish cream. In Yorkshire the puddings are often served before the meat, with the gravy, as a first course. Either way, this dish will have your guests asking for more.

Serves 6–8

rib of beef joint, weighing about 3kg/6½lb

oil, for brushing

salt and ground black pepper

For the Yorkshire puddings

115g/4oz/1 cup plain (all-purpose) flour

1.5ml/¼ tsp salt

1 egg

200ml/7fl oz/scant 1 cup milk

oil or beef dripping, for greasing

For the horseradish cream

60–75ml/4–5 tbsp finely grated fresh horseradish

300ml/½ pint/1¼ cups sour cream

30ml/2 tbsp cider vinegar or white wine vinegar

10ml/2 tsp caster (superfine) sugar

For the gravy

600ml/1 pint/2½ cups good beef stock

Cook's tip To avoid the pungent smell (and tears) produced by grating horseradish, use a jar of preserved grated horseradish.

1 Preheat the oven to 220°C/425°F/ Gas 7. Weigh the joint and calculate the cooking time required as follows: 10–15 minutes per 500g/1¼lb for rare beef, 15–20 minutes for medium and 20–25 minutes for well done.

2 Put the joint into a large roasting pan. Brush it all over with oil and season with salt and pepper. Put into the hot oven and cook for 30 minutes, until the beef is browned. Lower the oven temperature to 160°C/325°F/Gas 3 and cook for the calculated time, spooning the juices over the meat occasionally during cooking.

3 For the Yorkshire pudding, sift the flour and salt into a bowl and break the egg into it. Make the milk up to 300ml/½ pint/1¼ cups with water and gradually whisk into the flour to make a smooth batter. Leave to stand while the beef cooks. Generously grease eight Yorkshire pudding tins (muffin pans) measuring about 10cm/4in.

4 For the horseradish cream, put all the ingredients into a bowl and mix well. Cover and chill until required.

5 At the end of its cooking time, remove the beef from the oven, cover with foil and leave to stand for 30–40 minutes while you cook the Yorkshire puddings and make the gravy.

6 Increase the oven temperature to 220°C/425°F/Gas 7 and put the prepared tins on the top shelf for 5 minutes until very hot. Pour in the batter and cook for about 15 minutes until well risen, crisp and golden brown.

7 To make the gravy, transfer the beef to a warmed serving plate. Pour off the fat from the roasting pan, leaving the meat juices. Add the stock to the pan, bring to the boil and bubble until reduced by about half. Season to taste.

8 Carve the beef and serve with the gravy, Yorkshire puddings, roast potatoes and horseradish cream.

Per portion Energy 1037kcal/4338kJ; Protein 129g; Carbohydrate 15.1g, of which sugars 4.1g; Fat 51.5g, of which saturates 24.3g; Cholesterol 352mg; Calcium 123mg; Fibre 0.5g; Sodium 249mg.

Beef in red wine with a potato crust

This recipe makes the best of braising beef by marinating it in red wine and topping it with a cheesy grated potato crust that bakes to a golden, crunchy consistency. For a change, instead of grating the potatoes, slice them thinly and layer over the top of the beef with onion rings and crushed garlic. The dish makes a satistfying meal on its own.

Serves 4

675g/1½lb stewing beef, diced

300ml/½ pint/1¼ cups red wine

3 juniper berries, crushed

slice of orange peel

30ml/2 tbsp olive oil

2 onions, cut into chunks

2 carrots, cut into chunks

1 garlic clove, crushed

225g/8oz/3 cups button (white) mushrooms

150ml/¼ pint/⅔ cup beef stock

30ml/2 tbsp cornflour (cornstarch)

salt and ground black pepper

For the crust

450g/1lb potatoes, grated

15ml/1 tbsp olive oil

30ml/2 tbsp creamed horseradish

50g/2oz/½ cup mature (sharp) Cheddar cheese, grated

salt and ground black pepper

1 Place the diced beef in a non-metallic bowl. Add the wine, berries, and orange peel and season with pepper. Mix the ingredients, then cover and leave to marinate for at least 4 hours or overnight.

2 Preheat the oven to 160°C/325°F/Gas 3. Drain the beef, reserving the marinade.

3 Heat the oil in a large flameproof casserole and fry the meat in batches for 5 minutes to seal. Add the onions, carrots and garlic and cook for 5 minutes. Stir in the mushrooms, red wine marinade and beef stock. Simmer.

4 Mix the cornflour with water to make a smooth paste. Stir into the pan. Season, cover and cook for 1½ hours.

5 Make the crust 30 minutes before the end of the cooking time for the beef. Start by blanching the grated potatoes in boiling water for 5 minutes. Drain well and then squeeze out all the extra liquid.

6 Stir in the remaining ingredients and then sprinkle evenly over the surface of the beef. Increase the oven temperature to 200°C/400°F/Gas 6 and cook the dish for a further 30 minutes so that the top is crispy and slightly browned.

Cook's tip Use a large grater on the food processor for the potatoes, or alternatively, grate them by hand with a traditional grater. They will hold their shape better while being blanched than if you use a finer blade.

Per portion Energy 474kcal/1973kJ; Protein 43g; Carbohydrate 6.1g, of which sugars 5.6g; Fat 28.8g, of which saturates 8.7g; Cholesterol 106mg; Calcium 53mg; Fibre 2.6g; Sodium 564mg.

Steak and kidney pudding

One of the best-known English country dishes, this tasty pudding is a 19th-century recipe that originally contained oysters, but mushrooms are more often used today. Although it has a relatively long cooking time, the finished result is well worth the wait.

Serves 6

500g/1¼lb lean stewing steak, cut into cubes

225g/8oz beef kidney or lamb's kidneys, skin and core removed and cut into small cubes

1 medium onion, finely chopped

30ml/2 tbsp finely chopped fresh herbs, such as parsley and thyme

30ml/2 tbsp plain (all-purpose) flour

275g/10oz/2½ cups self-raising (self-rising) flour

150g/5oz/1 cup shredded suet (US chilled, grated shortening)

finely grated rind of 1 small lemon

about 120ml/4fl oz/½ cup beef stock or water

salt and ground black pepper

1 Put the stewing steak into a large bowl and add the kidneys, onion and chopped herbs. Sprinkle the plain flour and seasoning over the top and mix well.

2 To make the pastry, sift the self-raising flour into another large bowl. Stir in the suet and lemon rind. Add sufficient cold water to bind the ingredients and gather into a soft dough.

3 On a lightly floured surface, knead the dough gently, and then roll out to make a circle measuring about 35cm/14in across. Cut out one-quarter of the circle, roll up and put aside.

4 Lightly butter a 1.75 litre/3 pint heatproof bowl. Line the bowl with the rolled out dough, pressing the cut edges together and allowing the pastry to overlap the top of the bowl slightly.

5 Spoon the steak mixture into the lined bowl, packing it in carefully, so as not to split the pastry.

6 Pour in sufficient stock to reach no more than three-quarters of the way up the filling. (Any stock remaining can be heated and poured into the cooked pudding to thin the gravy if desired.)

7 Roll out the reserved pastry into a circle to form a lid and lay it over the filling, pinching the edges together to seal them well.

8 Cover with baking parchment, pleated in the centre to allow the pudding to rise, then cover again with a large sheet of foil (again pleated at the centre). Tuck the edges under and press them tightly to the sides of the basin until securely sealed (alternatively, tie with string). Steam for about 5 hours.

9 Carefully remove the foil and paper, slide a knife around the sides of the pudding and turn out on to a warmed serving plate.

Per portion Energy 436kcal/1835kJ; Protein 31.1g; Carbohydrate 49.5g, of which sugars 4.8g; Fat 13.9g, of which saturates 3.6g; Cholesterol 166mg; Calcium 201mg; Fibre 1.9g; Sodium 380mg.

Veal casserole with broad beans

This delicate stew, flavoured with sherry and plenty of garlic, is a spring casserole made with new vegetables. For a delicious flavour, add plenty of parsley before serving.

Serves 6

45ml/3 tbsp olive oil

1.3–1.6kg/3–3½lb veal, cut into 5cm/2in cubes

1 large onion, chopped

6 large garlic cloves, unpeeled

1 bay leaf

5ml/1 tsp paprika

250ml/8fl oz/1 cup fino sherry

100g/4oz/scant 1 cup shelled, skinned broad (fava) beans

60ml/4 tbsp fresh flat leaf parsley

salt and ground black pepper

1 Heat 30ml/2 tbsp oil in a large flameproof casserole. Add half the meat and brown well on all sides. Transfer to a plate. Brown the rest of the meat and remove from the pan.

2 Add the remaining oil to the pan and cook the onion until soft. Return the meat to the casserole and stir well to mix with the onion.

3 Add the garlic cloves, bay leaf, paprika and sherry. Season. Bring to simmering point, then cover and cook very gently for 30–40 minutes.

4 Add the broad beans to the casserole about 10 minutes before the end of the cooking time. Chop the flat leaf parsley. Check the seasoning and stir in the parsley just before serving.

Per portion Energy 352kcal/1473kJ; Protein 47.4g; Carbohydrate 3.6g, of which sugars 1.3g; Fat 11.6g, of which saturates 2.8g; Cholesterol 182mg; Calcium 34mg; Fibre 1.2g; Sodium 244mg.

Rustic meat loaf

Made with beef, pork and veal mince, this tasty meat loaf has plenty of fresh herbs and seasoning, and is lovely served with a home-made tomato sauce.

Serves 6

25g/1oz/2 tbsp butter or margarine

1 onion, finely chopped

2 garlic cloves, finely chopped

50g/2oz/½ cup finely chopped celery

450g/1lb lean ground beef

225g/8oz veal mince

225g/8oz lean pork mince

2 eggs

50g/2oz/1 cup fine fresh breadcrumbs

25g/1oz/½ cup chopped fresh parsley

30ml/2 tbsp chopped fresh basil

2.5ml/½ tsp fresh or dried thyme leaves

2.5ml/½ tsp salt

2.5ml/½ tsp pepper

30ml/2 tbsp Worcestershire sauce

50ml/2fl oz/¼ cup chilli sauce or tomato ketchup

6 bacon rashers (strips)

1 Preheat oven to 180°C/350°F/Gas 4. Melt the butter or margarine in a small frying pan over a low heat. Add the onion, garlic and celery and cook until softened, 8–10 minutes. Remove from the heat and leave to cool slightly.

2 In a large mixing bowl, combine the onion, garlic and celery with all the other ingredients except the bacon. Mix together lightly, using a fork or your fingers. Do not overwork or the meat loaf will be too compact.

3 Form the meat mixture into an oval loaf. Carefully transfer it to a shallow baking tin (pan).

4 Lay the bacon across the meat loaf. Bake for 1¼ hours, basting occasionally with the juices and bacon fat in the pan.

5 Remove from the oven and drain off the fat. Leave the meat loaf to stand for 10 minutes before serving. Carefully lift the meat loaf on to a serving dish and slice thickly.

Per portion Energy 286kcal/1189kJ; Protein 18.6g; Carbohydrate 11.9g, of which sugars 5.1g; Fat 18.5g, of which saturates 8.3g; Cholesterol 119mg; Calcium 62mg; Fibre 1g; Sodium 572mg.

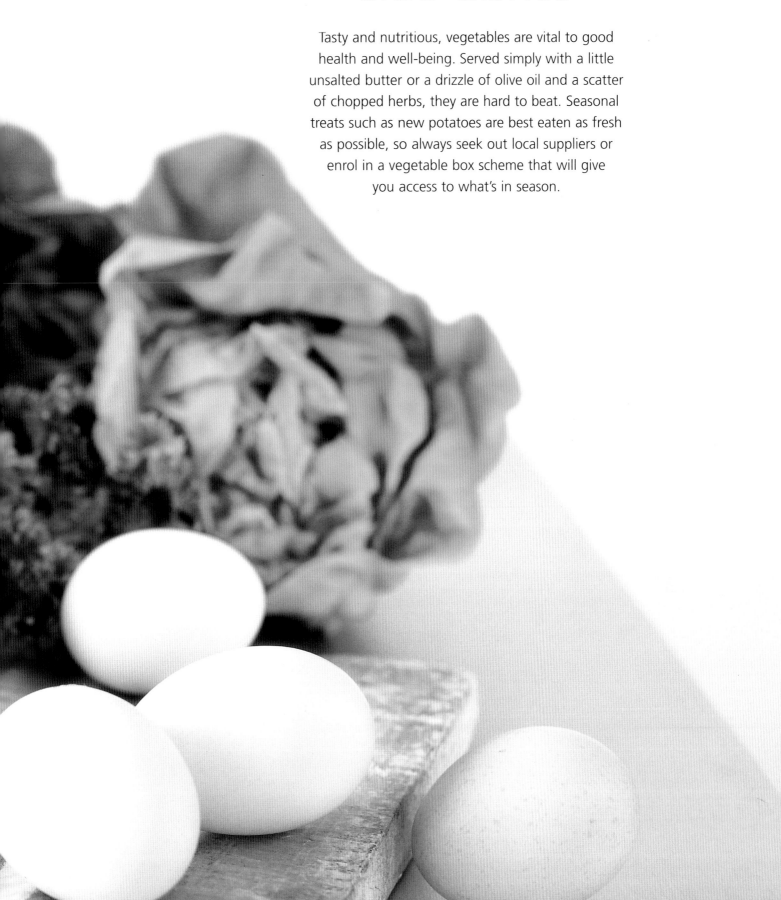

Vegetable side dishes

Tasty and nutritious, vegetables are vital to good health and well-being. Served simply with a little unsalted butter or a drizzle of olive oil and a scatter of chopped herbs, they are hard to beat. Seasonal treats such as new potatoes are best eaten as fresh as possible, so always seek out local suppliers or enrol in a vegetable box scheme that will give you access to what's in season.

Creamed leeks

Versatile leeks are a great winter vegetable, adding a subtle onion flavour to many dishes, including soups, casseroles, stews and stir-fries. Serve these creamed leeks on their own, or as a tasty accompaniment to grilled meats, such as chops, chicken or gammon.

Serves 4–6

4 large or 8 medium leeks

300ml/½ pint/1¼ cups milk

8 streaky (fatty) rashers (strips) of bacon, trimmed and sliced (optional)

1 egg, lightly beaten

150ml/¼ pint/⅔ cup single (light) cream

15ml/1 tbsp mild Irish mustard

75g/3oz/¾ cup grated cheese (optional)

salt and ground black pepper

1 Slice the leeks into fairly large chunks. Put them into a pan with the milk. Season and bring to the boil. Reduce the heat and simmer for 15–20 minutes, or until tender. Drain well and turn the leeks into a buttered shallow baking dish, reserving the cooking liquor.

2 Meanwhile, if using the bacon, put it into a frying pan and cook gently to allow the fat to run, then turn up the heat a little and cook for a few minutes until it crisps up. Remove from the pan with a slotted spoon and sprinkle the bacon over the leeks.

3 Rinse the pan used for the leeks. Blend the beaten egg, single cream and Irish mustard together and mix it with the reserved cooking liquor. Return to the pan and heat gently without boiling, allowing the sauce to thicken a little. Taste and adjust the seasoning with salt and ground black pepper. Pour the sauce over the leeks and bacon.

4 Sprinkle the baking dish with grated cheese, if using, and brown for a few minutes under a hot grill (broiler). (Alternatively, the leeks may be served immediately without browning them.) Serve with plain grilled (broiled) meat or poultry, if you like.

Variations
• The bacon may be grilled (broiled) and served separately, if you prefer.
• Omit the cheese topping and use the leeks and bacon to dress hot tagliatelle or spaghetti, or use in a risotto.
• The leeks could also be spread on to toast topped with cheese and grilled for a light lunch.

Per portion Energy 238kcal/993kJ; Protein 18.6g; Carbohydrate 9g, of which sugars 7.9g; Fat 14.4g, of which saturates 7.3g; Cholesterol 90mg; Calcium 172mg; Fibre 3.5g; Sodium 830mg.

Sautéed broad beans with bacon

The texture and flavour of broad beans is perfectly complemented by bacon. Broad beans are sweeter and more tender in the earlier part of the season, so use young beans in this recipe or, if using larger beans, remove the skins to reveal the bright green inner bean.

Serves 4

30ml/2 tbsp olive oil

1 small onion, finely chopped

1 garlic clove, finely chopped

50g/2oz rindless smoked streaky (fatty) bacon, roughly chopped

225g/8oz broad (fava) beans, thawed if frozen

5ml/1 tsp paprika

15ml/1 tbsp sweet sherry

salt and ground black pepper

1 Heat the olive oil in a large frying pan or sauté pan. Add the chopped onion, garlic and bacon and fry over a high heat for about 5 minutes, stirring frequently, until the onion is softened and the bacon browned.

2 Add the beans and paprika to the pan and stir-fry for 1 minute. Add the sherry, lower the heat, cover and cook for 5–10 minutes until the beans are tender. Season with salt and pepper to taste and serve hot or warm.

Per portion Energy 139kcal/577kJ; Protein 6.8g; Carbohydrate 8.2g, of which sugars 1.6g; Fat 9g, of which saturates 1.9g; Cholesterol 8mg; Calcium 38mg; Fibre 3.9g; Sodium 163mg.

Carrot and parsnip purée

The most widely used and versatile of root vegetables, carrots blend beautifully with all the others. In this easy-to-make recipe they are mashed together with tasty parsnips, creating a smooth and flavourful combination. Celeriac, swede or sweet potatoes all purée well too.

Serves 6–8

350g/12oz carrots

450g/1lb parsnips

pinch of freshly grated nutmeg or ground mace

15g/½oz/1 tbsp butter

about 15ml/1 tbsp single (light) cream, or top of the milk (optional)

1 small bunch parsley leaves, chopped (optional), plus extra to garnish

salt and ground black pepper

1 Peel the carrots and slice fairly thinly. Peel the parsnips and cut into bitesize chunks (they are softer and will cook more quickly than the carrots). Boil the two vegetables, separately, in salted water, until tender.

2 Drain them well and put them through a mouli-légumes (food mill) with the grated nutmeg or mace, a good seasoning of salt and ground black pepper and the butter. Purée together and taste for seasoning.

▶ **3** If you like, blend in some cream or top of the milk to taste, and add chopped parsley for extra flavour.

4 Transfer the carrot and parsnip purée to a warmed serving bowl, sprinkle with freshly chopped parsley to garnish and serve hot.

Cook's tip Any leftover purée can be thinned to taste with good-quality chicken stock and heated to make a quick home-made soup.

Per portion Energy 92kcal/385kJ; Protein 1.8g; Carbohydrate 14.1g, of which sugars 8.7g; Fat 3.5g, of which saturates 1.8g; Cholesterol 7mg; Calcium 48mg; Fibre 4.9g; Sodium 38mg

Spiced red cabbage with apple

A hardy vegetable, red cabbage can be grown in tough conditions – it was ubiquitous in the European rural diet, and especially popular throughout Germany. This colourful, sharp and sweet-flavoured side dish is ideal served alongside roast pork, goose and game.

Serves 4–6

1kg/2¼lb red cabbage

2 cooking apples

2 onions, chopped

5ml/1 tsp freshly grated nutmeg

1.5ml/¼ tsp ground cloves

1.5ml/¼ tsp ground cinnamon

15ml/1 tbsp soft dark brown sugar

45ml/3 tbsp red wine vinegar

25g/1oz/2 tbsp butter, diced

salt and ground black pepper

chopped flat leaf parsley, to garnish

2 Layer the shredded cabbage in a large ovenproof dish with the onions, apples, spices, sugar, and salt and ground black pepper. Pour over the vinegar and add the diced butter.

3 Cover the dish with a lid and cook in the preheated oven for about 1½ hours, stirring a couple of times, until the cabbage is very tender. Serve immediately, garnished with the parsley.

1 Preheat the oven to 160°C/325°F/ Gas 3. Cut away and discard the large white ribs from the outer cabbage leaves using a large, sharp knife, then finely shred the cabbage. Peel, core and coarsely grate the apples.

Cook's tip This dish can be cooked in advance. Bake the cabbage for 1½ hours, then leave to cool. Store in a cool place covered with clear film (plastic wrap). To complete the cooking, bake it in the oven at 160°C/325°F/Gas 3 for about 30 minutes, stirring occasionally.

Per portion Energy 160kcal/668kJ; Protein 4.3g; Carbohydrate 23.8g, of which sugars 22.4g; Fat 5.8g, of which saturates 3.3g; Cholesterol 13mg; Calcium 140mg; Fibre 6.6g; Sodium 58mg.

Oven-roast red onions

Serve these sticky, sweet and fragrant onions with roast chicken or warm as part of a mezze. Alternatively, crumble over some fresh herb cheese and serve with crusty bread.

Serves 4

4 large or 8 small red onions

45ml/3 tbsp olive oil

6 juniper berries, crushed

8 small rosemary sprigs

30ml/2 tbsp balsamic vinegar

salt and ground black pepper

Cook's tips

• To help hold back the tears, chill the onions first for about 30 minutes, then remove the root end last. The root contains the largest concentration of the sulphuric compounds that make the eyes water.

• If you don't have an onion baker, use a ceramic baking dish and cover with foil.

1 Soak a clay onion baker in cold water for 15 minutes, then drain. If the base of the baker is glazed, only the lid will need to be soaked.

2 Cut the onions from the tip to the root, cutting the large onions into quarters and the small onions in half. Trim the roots from the onions and remove the skins, if you like.

3 Rub the onions with olive oil, salt and pepper and the juniper berries. Place the onions in the baker, inserting the rosemary in among the onions. Pour the remaining olive oil and vinegar over.

4 Cover and place in an unheated oven. Set the oven to 200°C/400°F/Gas 6 and cook for 40 minutes. Remove the lid and cook for a further 10 minutes.

Per portion Energy 128kcal/530kJ; Protein 1.8g; Carbohydrate 11.9g, of which sugars 8.4g; Fat 8.6g, of which saturates 1.2g; Cholesterol 0mg; Calcium 38mg; Fibre 2.1g; Sodium 5mg.

Baked tomatoes with mint

This is a high summer recipe that makes the most of falling-off-the-vine ripe tomatoes and fresh mint. Serve this attractive dish with grilled lamb or fish. It is ideal for a barbecue.

Serves 4

6 large ripe tomatoes

300ml/½ pint/1¼ cups double (heavy) cream

2 sprigs of fresh mint

olive oil, for brushing

a few pinches of caster (superfine) sugar

30ml/2 tbsp grated Bonnet cheese

salt and ground black pepper

Cook's tip Bonnet is a hard variety of goat's cheese but any other hard, well-flavoured cheese will do.

1 Preheat the oven to 220°C/425°F/ Gas 7. Bring a pan of water to the boil and have a bowl of iced water ready. Cut the cores out of the tomatoes and make a cross at the base. Plunge the tomatoes into the boiling water for 10 seconds and then straight into the iced water. Leave to cool completely.

2 Put the cream and mint in a pan and bring to the boil. Reduce the heat and allow to simmer until it has reduced by about half.

3 Peel the cooled tomatoes and slice them thinly. Pat dry on kitchen paper.

4 Brush a shallow gratin dish lightly with a little olive oil. Layer the sliced tomatoes in the dish, overlapping slightly, and season with salt and ground black pepper. Sprinkle a little sugar over the top.

5 Strain the reduced cream evenly over the top of the tomatoes. Sprinkle on the cheese and bake in the preheated oven for 15 minutes, or until the top is browned and bubbling. Serve immediately in the gratin dish.

Per portion Energy 443kcal/1831kJ; Protein 5g; Carbohydrate 6.7g, of which sugars 6.7g; Fat 44.1g, of which saturates 27.4g; Cholesterol 113mg; Calcium 123mg; Fibre 1.8g; Sodium 105mg.

Farmhouse cheese-baked courgettes

This is an easy dish that makes a great accompaniment to a wide range of meat and fish dishes or a good vegetarian lunch. Use piquant farmhouse cheddar or mature goat's cheese.

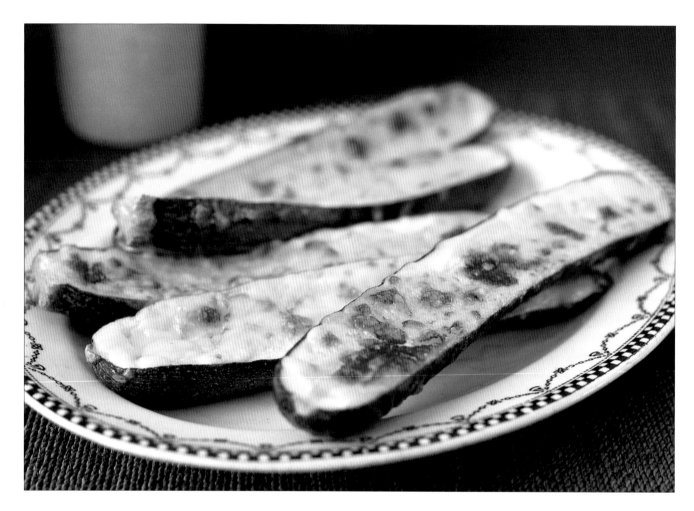

Serves 4

4 courgettes (zucchini)

30ml/2 tbsp grated hard farmhouse cheese, such as Gabriel or Desmond

about 25g/1oz/2 tbsp butter

salt and ground black pepper

1 Preheat the oven to 180°C/350°F/ Gas 4. Slice the courgettes in half, lengthways. Trim the ends and discard.

2 Butter a shallow baking dish and arrange the courgettes, cut side up, inside the dish.

3 Sprinkle the cheese over the courgettes, and sprinkle over a few knobs (pats) of butter. Bake in the preheated oven for about 20 minutes, or until the courgettes are tender and the cheese is bubbling and golden brown. Serve immediately.

Per portion Energy 96kcal/395kJ; Protein 3.8g; Carbohydrate 1.9g, of which sugars 1.8g; Fat 8g, of which saturates 5g; Cholesterol 21mg; Calcium 82mg; Fibre 0.9g; Sodium 93mg.

Courgette and potato bake

This is an early autumn dish. Serve the oven-baked courgettes with bread, olives and grilled lamb, feta or halloumi cheese for a satisfying vegetarian meal.

Serves 6

675g/1½lb courgettes (zucchini)

450g/1lb potatoes, peeled and cut into chunks

1 onion, finely sliced

3 garlic cloves, chopped

1 large red (bell) pepper, seeded and cubed

400g/14oz can chopped tomatoes

150ml/¼ pint/⅔ cup extra virgin olive oil

150ml/¼ pint/⅔ cup hot water

5ml/1 tsp dried oregano

45ml/3 tbsp chopped fresh flat leaf parsley, plus a few extra sprigs, to garnish

salt and ground black pepper

1 Preheat the oven to 190°C/375°F/ Gas 5. Scrape the courgettes lightly under running water to dislodge any grit and then slice them into thin rounds. Put them in a large baking dish and add the chopped potatoes, onion, garlic, red pepper and tomatoes.

2 Mix well, then stir in the olive oil, hot water and dried oregano.

3 Spread the mixture evenly, then season with salt and pepper. Bake for 30 minutes, then stir in the parsley and a little more water.

4 Return to the oven and cook for 1 hour, increasing the temperature to 200°C/400°F/Gas 6 for the final 10–15 minutes, so that the potatoes brown.

Per portion Energy 374kcal/1,554kJ; Protein 6.6g; Carbohydrate 28.6g, of which sugars 11.2g; Fat 26.7g, of which saturates 4g; Cholesterol 0mg; Calcium 86mg; Fibre 5.1g; Sodium 29mg.

New potato salad with chives

The potatoes in this dish absorb the oil and vinegar dressing as they cool, and are then tossed in mayonnaise. Small waxy potatoes, which can be kept whole, are particularly suitable for this recipe. Serve them with cold poached salmon or roast chicken.

2 Meanwhile, finely chop the white parts of the spring onions together with a little of the green part.

3 Whisk the oil with the vinegar and mustard. Drain the potatoes. Immediately, while the potatoes are still hot and steaming, toss them lightly with the oil mixture and the spring onions. Leave to cool.

Serves 4–6

675g/1½lb small new potatoes, unpeeled

4 spring onions (scallions)

45ml/3 tbsp olive oil

15ml/1 tbsp cider vinegar or wine vinegar

2.5ml/½ tsp ready-made English (hot) mustard

175ml/6fl oz/¾ cup mayonnaise

45ml/3 tbsp chopped fresh chives

salt and ground black pepper

Variation Add a handful of chopped parsley or mint to the salad with the mayonnaise instead of chives.

1 Cook the new potatoes in boiling salted water for about 15 minutes, or until tender.

4 Stir the mayonnaise and chives into the cooled potatoes and turn into a serving bowl. Chill the salad until you are ready to serve.

Per portion Energy 182kcal/761kJ; Protein 2.5g; Carbohydrate 22.5g, of which sugars 1.9g; Fat 9.7g, of which saturates 1.5g; Cholesterol 0mg; Calcium 20mg; Fibre 1.7g; Sodium 17mg.

Vine tomato salad with peppers and oregano

Home-grown tomatoes fresh from the vine would be ideal here, but any ripe, juicy fruits combined with the marinated peppers would make a lovely appetizer or side dish for a summer buffet. Sprinkle over a few fresh basil leaves instead of the oregano, if you prefer.

Serves 4–6

2 marinated (bell) peppers, drained

6 ripe tomatoes, sliced

15ml/1 tbsp chopped fresh oregano

75ml/5 tbsp olive oil

30ml/2 tbsp white wine vinegar

sea salt

Cook's tip To marinate (bell) peppers, wrap one green and one red pepper in foil and place on a baking sheet. Cook in a preheated oven at 180°C/350°F/Gas 4, or under a preheated grill (broiler), turning occasionally, for 20–30 minutes, until tender. Unwrap and when cool, peel the peppers, then halve and seed. Cut the flesh into strips and pack into a screw-top jar. Add olive oil to cover, close and store in the refrigerator for up to 6 days.

1 If the marinated peppers are in large pieces, cut them into strips. Arrange the tomato slices and pepper strips on a serving dish, sprinkle with the oregano and season to taste with sea salt.

2 Whisk together the olive oil and vinegar in a jug (pitcher), decant into a bottle and pour the dressing over the salad. Serve immediately or cover and chill in the refrigerator until required.

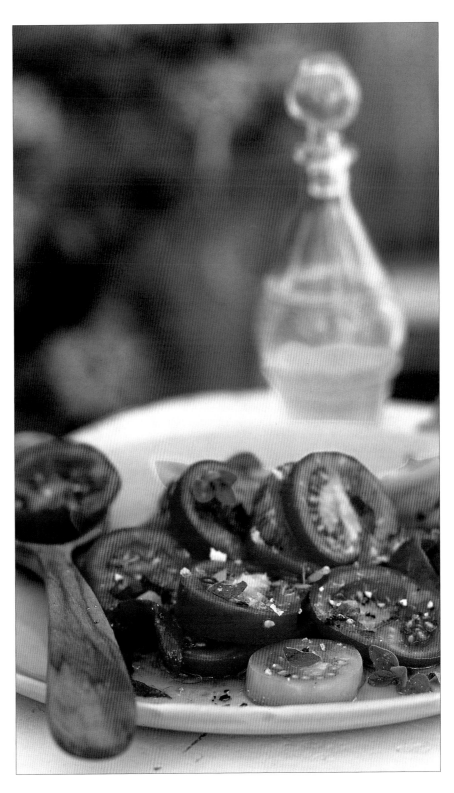

Per portion Energy 119kcal/494kJ; Protein 1.4g; Carbohydrate 6.9g, of which sugars 6.7g; Fat 9.7g, of which saturates 1.5g; Cholesterol 0mg; Calcium 17mg; Fibre 2.1g; Sodium 12mg.

Puddings and desserts

The aroma of a gently steaming pudding is a delectable part of winter country cooking, while the abundant fruits of summer make luscious desserts. This chapter includes warm favourites such as winter fruit crumble and rice pudding, dishes that make use of hedgerow and orchard fruits such as apple pie and chilled berry pudding, and economical staples such as bread and butter pudding.

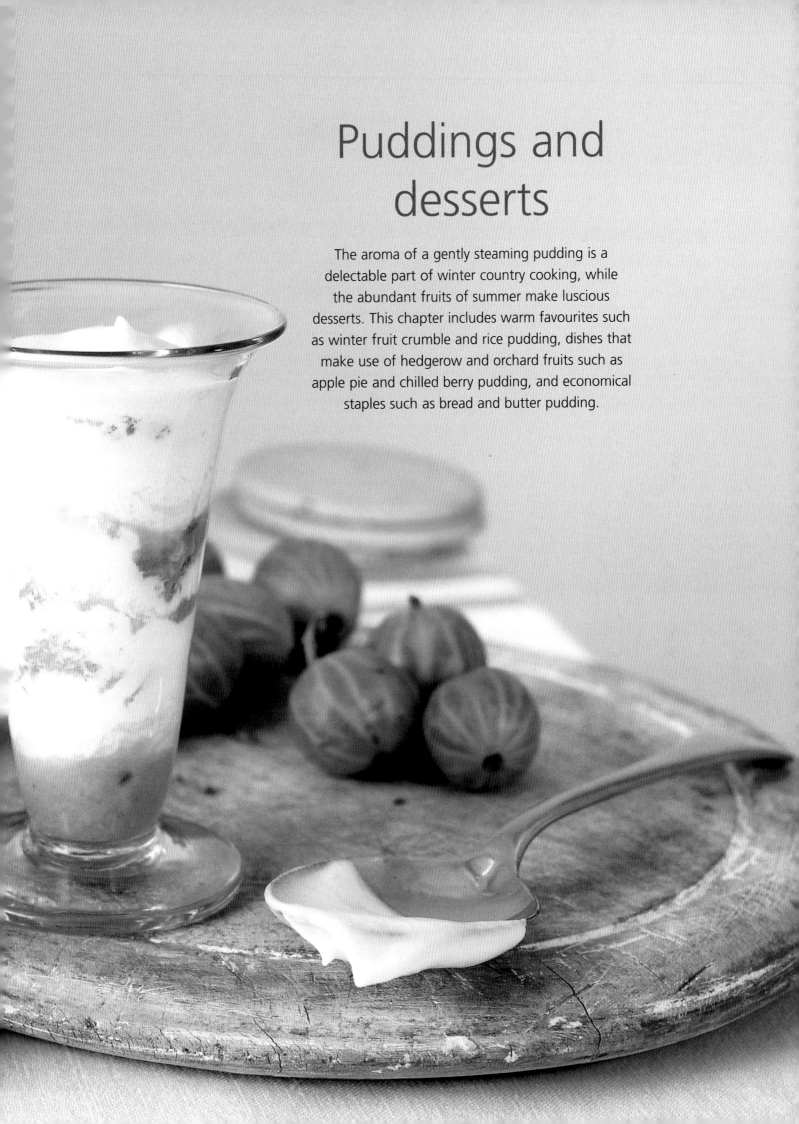

Hot bramble and apple soufflés

Hedgerow brambles, blackberries, loganberries or blackcurrants would all work equally well in this deliciously light pudding. Serve with lashings of thick cream or crème anglais.

Makes 6

butter, for greasing

150g/5oz/¾ cup caster (superfine) sugar, plus extra for dusting

350g/12oz/3 cups blackberries

1 large cooking apple, peeled and finely diced

grated rind and juice of 1 orange

3 egg whites

icing (confectioners') sugar, for dusting

1 Preheat the oven to 200°C/400°F/ Gas 6. Generously grease six 150ml/ ¼ pint/⅔ cup individual soufflé dishes with butter and dust with caster sugar, shaking out the excess sugar.

2 Put a baking sheet in the oven to heat. Cook the blackberries, diced apple and orange rind and juice in a pan for 10 minutes or until the apple has pulped down well.

3 Press through a sieve (strainer) into a bowl. Stir in 50g/2oz/¼ cup of the caster sugar. Set aside to cool for about 20–30 minutes.

4 Put a spoonful of the fruit purée into each prepared dish and smooth the surface. Set the dishes aside.

5 Whisk the egg whites in a large grease-free bowl until they form stiff peaks. Very gradually whisk in the remaining caster sugar to make a stiff, glossy meringue mixture.

6 Fold in the remaining fruit purée and spoon the flavoured meringue into the prepared dishes. Level the tops with a palette knife, and run a table knife around the edge of each dish.

7 Place the dishes on the hot baking sheet and bake for 10–15 minutes until the soufflés have risen well and are lightly browned. Dust the tops with icing sugar and serve immediately.

Cook's tip Running a table knife around the inside edge of the dishes before baking helps the soufflés to rise evenly without sticking to the rim.

Per portion Energy 123kcal/522kJ; Protein 2.1g; Carbohydrate 30.1g, of which sugars 30.1g; Fat 0.1g, of which saturates 0g; Cholesterol 0mg; Calcium 38mg; Fibre 2g; Sodium 33mg.

Autumn orchard pudding

This autumn version of a summer pudding makes the most of seasonal orchard fruits.
Serve with cream, lightly whipped with apple brandy or plain crème fraîche.

Serves 6–8

1 loaf white bread, 2 or 3 days old

675g/1½lb/6 cups mixed soft fruit, such as blackberries, autumn raspberries, late strawberries, and peeled and chopped eating apples

115g/4oz/generous ½ cup caster (superfine) sugar or 75ml/5 tbsp honey

1 Remove the crusts from the loaf and slice the bread thinly. Use several slices to line the base and sides of a 900ml–1.2 litre/1½–2 pint/3¾–5 cup pudding bowl or soufflé dish, cutting them carefully so that the pieces fit closely together.

2 Put all the fruit into a wide, heavy pan, sprinkle the sugar or honey over and bring very gently to the boil. Cook for 2–3 minutes, or until the sugar has dissolved and the juices run.

3 Remove the pan from the heat and set aside 30–45ml/2–3 tbsp of the juices. Spoon the fruit and the remaining juices into the prepared bread-lined dish and cover the top closely with the remaining slices of bread. Put a plate that fits neatly inside the top of the dish on top of the pudding and weigh it down with a heavy tin or jar. Leave in the refrigerator for at least 8 hours, or overnight.

4 Before serving the dish, remove the weight and plate, cover the bowl with a serving plate and turn upside down to unmould the pudding.

5 Use the reserved fruit juice to pour over any patches of the bread that have not been completely soaked and coloured by the fruit juices. Serve cold cut into wedges with lightly whipped chilled cream or crème fraîche.

Per portion Energy 261kcal/1112kJ; Protein 7.7g; Carbohydrate 57.5g, of which sugars 27.1g; Fat 1.7g, of which saturates 0.4g; Cholesterol 0mg; Calcium 153mg; Fibre 4.2g; Sodium 398mg.

Sticky honey and ginger baked apples

Baked apples are a country-cooking staple, and there are myriad different versions – they can be made with any type of eating apple and stuffed with vine fruits, spices and citrus fruits. This version uses honey and fresh ginger, and is accompanied by either vanilla sauce, sour cream or double cream. A final touch of luxury would be to fold a little whipped cream into the vanilla sauce before serving, then spooning stem ginger ice cream on top.

Serves 4

4 eating apples, such as Cox's Orange Pippin or Golden Delicious

30ml/2 tbsp finely chopped fresh root ginger

60ml/4 tbsp honey

25g/1oz/2 tbsp unsalted (sweet) butter

60ml/4 tbsp medium white wine

vanilla sauce, sour cream or double (heavy) cream, to serve

For the vanilla sauce

300ml/½ pint/1¼ cups single (light) cream

1 vanilla pod (bean), split lengthways

2 egg yolks

30ml/2 tbsp caster (superfine) sugar

1 To make the vanilla sauce, put the cream and vanilla pod in a pan and heat to just below boiling point. Remove from the heat and leave to infuse for 10 minutes. Remove the vanilla pod.

2 Put the egg yolks and sugar in a bowl and whisk them together until pale and thick, then slowly pour in the cream, whisking all the time.

3 Return the pan to the heat and heat very gently until the cream is thick enough to coat the back of a wooden spoon. (If you draw a finger horizontally across the back of the spoon, the sauce should be thick enough not to run down through the channel.)

4 Remove from the heat and leave to cool. Either stir from time to time, or cover to prevent a skin forming.

5 Preheat the oven to 160°C/325°F/ Gas 3. Remove the cores from the apples leaving the stalk end intact, but remove the actual stalk. Fill each cavity with 2.5ml/½ tbsp chopped ginger and 15ml/1 tbsp honey.

6 Place the apples in an ovenproof dish, with the open end uppermost, and top each one with a knob of butter.

7 Pour in the wine and bake in the oven, basting frequently with the cooking juices, for about 45 minutes, until the apples are tender. Serve the apples with the vanilla sauce, sour cream or double cream.

Cook's tip If the sauce looks as though it may overheat, plunge the base of the pan into a bowl of cold water. This will cool the contents and prevent it curdling.

Per portion Energy 331kcal/1381kJ; Protein 4.3g; Carbohydrate 27.8g, of which sugars 27.8g; Fat 22.3g, of which saturates 13.2g; Cholesterol 155mg; Calcium 89mg; Fibre 1.2g; Sodium 68mg.

Maple and pecan steamed pudding

Imagine a hot sponge cake, straight out of the oven but with less golden crust, a deeper sponge and more crumbliness – that's a steamed pudding. It can be flavoured with anything; maple syrup and pecan nuts are wonderful. Serve with home-made custard.

Serves 6

60ml/4 tbsp pure maple syrup

30ml/2 tbsp fresh brown breadcrumbs

115g/4oz/1 cup shelled pecan nuts, roughly chopped

115g/4oz/½ cup butter, softened

finely grated rind of 1 orange

115g/4oz/heaped ½ cup golden caster (superfine) sugar

2 eggs, beaten

175g/6oz/1½ cups self-raising (self-rising) flour, sifted

pinch of salt

about 75ml/5 tbsp milk

extra maple syrup and home-made custard, to serve

1 Butter a 900ml/1½ pint/3¾ cup heatproof pudding bowl generously. Stir the maple syrup, breadcrumbs and pecans together and spoon into the bowl.

2 Cream the butter with the orange rind and sugar until light and fluffy. Gradually beat in the eggs, then fold in the flour and salt. Stir in enough milk to make a loose mixture that will drop off the spoon if lightly shaken.

3 Carefully spoon the mixture into the bowl on top of the syrup and nuts. Cover with pleated, buttered baking parchment, then with pleated foil (the pleats allow for expansion). Tie string under the lip of the basin to hold the paper in place, then take it over the top to form a handle.

4 Place the bowl in a pan of simmering water, cover and steam for 2 hours, topping up with boiling water as necessary.

5 Remove the string, foil and paper, then turn out the pudding and serve with extra maple syrup and a spoonful of home-made custard.

Per portion Energy 523kcal/2187kJ; Protein 7.7g; Carbohydrate 55.6g, of which sugars 29.9g; Fat 31.6g, of which saturates 12.2g; Cholesterol 108mg; Calcium 160mg; Fibre 1.9g; Sodium 345mg.

Winter fruit crumble

This recipe uses pears and dried fruits under the crumble topping, making it a deliciously warming winter pudding. At other times of the year, try gooseberries or rhubarb flavoured with orange rind. The almond topping adds a wonderfully rich texture.

Serves 6

175g/6oz/1½ cups plain (all-purpose) flour

50g/2oz/½ cup ground almonds

175g/6oz/¾ cup butter, diced

115g/4oz/½ cup soft light brown sugar

40g/1½oz flaked (sliced) almonds

1 orange

about 16 ready-to-eat dried apricots

4 firm ripe pears

1 Preheat the oven to 190°C/375°F/ Gas 5. To make the topping, sift the flour into a bowl and stir in the ground almonds. Add the butter and rub it into the flour until the mixture resembles rough breadcrumbs. Stir in 75g/3oz/ ⅓ cup sugar and the flaked almonds.

2 Finely grate 5ml/1 tsp rind from the orange and squeeze out its juice. Halve the apricots and put them into a shallow ovenproof dish. Peel the pears, remove their cores and cut the fruit into small pieces. Sprinkle the pears over the apricots. Stir the orange rind into the orange juice and sprinkle over the fruit. Sprinkle the remaining brown sugar over the top.

3 Cover the fruit completely with the crumble mixture and smooth over. Put into the hot oven and cook for about 40 minutes until the topping is golden brown and the fruit is soft (test with the point of a sharp knife).

Per portion Energy 615kcal/2569kJ; Protein 9.4g; Carbohydrate 65.7g, of which sugars 42.9g; Fat 36.7g, of which saturates 16.2g; Cholesterol 62mg; Calcium 150mg; Fibre 6.6g; Sodium 190mg.

Rice pudding with nutmeg

Originally a medieval treat at a time when rice and sugar were expensive imports, rice pudding went on to become a Victorian country favourite. This simple pudding can be enlivened by adding a spoonful of preserves or some brandy-soaked dried vine fruits or figs.

Serves 4

50g/2oz/4 tbsp butter, diced, plus extra for greasing

50g/2oz/¼ cup pudding rice

30ml/2 tbsp soft light brown sugar

900ml/1½ pints/3¾ cups milk

small strip of lemon rind

freshly grated nutmeg

Variation Add some sultanas (golden raisins), raisins or ready-to-eat dried apricots and cinnamon to the pudding.

Cook's tip Serve with fresh fruit such as peaches, raspberries or strawberries.

1 Preheat the oven to 150°C/300°F/ Gas 2. Butter a 1.2 litre/2 pint/5 cup shallow ovenproof dish.

2 Put the rice, sugar and butter into the dish and stir in the milk. Add the strip of lemon rind and sprinkle a little nutmeg over the surface. Put the pudding into the hot oven.

3 Cook the pudding for about 2 hours, stirring after 30 minutes and another couple of times during the next 1½ hours, until the rice is tender and the pudding is thick and creamy.

4 If you prefer skin on top, leave the pudding undisturbed for the final 30 minutes, or stir again. Serve with jam.

Per portion Energy 298kcal/1252kJ; Protein 8.8g; Carbohydrate 54.3g, of which sugars 21.5g; Fat 5.2g, of which saturates 1.4g; Cholesterol 143mg; Calcium 71mg; Fibre 0g; Sodium 185mg.

Bread and butter pudding with whiskey sauce

The ultimate comfort food and made to use up stale bread, this dish becomes rather sophisticated with the addition of a boozy whiskey sauce. It is best served with vanilla ice cream or chilled cream – the contrast between the hot and cold is exquisite.

Serves 6

8 slices of white bread, buttered

115–150g/4–5oz/²⁄₃–³⁄₄ cup sultanas (golden raisins), or mixed dried fruit

2.5ml/½ tsp grated nutmeg

150g/5oz/³⁄₄ cup caster (superfine) sugar

2 large (US extra large) eggs

300ml/½ pint/1¼ cups single (light) cream

450ml/³⁄₄ pint/scant 2 cups milk

5ml/1 tsp of vanilla extract

light muscovado (brown) sugar, for sprinkling (optional)

For the whiskey sauce

150g/5oz/10 tbsp butter

115g/4oz/generous ½ cup caster (superfine) sugar

1 egg

45ml/3 tbsp Irish whiskey

1 Preheat the oven to 180°C/350°F/ Gas 4. Remove the crusts from the bread and put four slices, buttered side down, in the base of an ovenproof dish. Sprinkle with the fruit, some of the nutmeg and 15ml/1 tbsp sugar.

2 Place the remaining four slices of bread on top, buttered side down, and sprinkle again with nutmeg and 15ml/1 tbsp sugar.

3 Beat the eggs lightly, add the cream, milk, vanilla extract and the remaining sugar, and mix well to make a custard. Pour this mixture over the bread, and sprinkle light muscovado sugar over the top, if you like to have a crispy crust.

4 Bake in the preheated oven for 1 hour, or until all the liquid has been absorbed and the pudding is risen and brown.

5 Meanwhile, make the whiskey sauce: melt the butter in a heavy pan, add the caster sugar and dissolve over gentle heat. Remove from the heat and add the egg, whisking vigorously, and then add the whiskey. Serve the pudding on hot serving plates, with the whiskey sauce poured over the top.

Per portion Energy 757kcal/3168kJ; Protein 11.7g; Carbohydrate 82g, of which sugars 65.2g; Fat 40.8g, of which saturates 24.3g; Cholesterol 207mg; Calcium 232mg; Fibre 0.9g; Sodium 472mg.

Black cherry clafoutis

Clafoutis is a batter pudding that originated in the Limousin area of central France.
It is often made with cream and traditionally uses slightly tart black cherries, although
other soft fruits such as halved apricots, peaches or plums will also give delicious results.

Serves 6

butter, for greasing

450g/1lb/2 cups black cherries, pitted

25g/1oz/¼ cup plain (all-purpose) flour

50g/2oz/½ cup icing (confectioners')
sugar, plus extra for dusting

4 eggs, beaten

250ml/8fl oz/1 cup full-cream
(whole) milk

30ml/2 tbsp cherry liqueur,
such as kirsch or maraschino

1 Preheat the oven to 180°C/350°F/
Gas 4. Generously grease a 1.2 litre/
2 pint/5 cup dish and add the pitted
black cherries.

2 Sift the flour and icing sugar into a
large mixing bowl, then gradually whisk
in the beaten eggs until the mixture is
smooth. Whisk in the milk until well
blended, then stir in the liqueur.

3 Pour the batter into the baking dish.
Transfer to the oven and bake for about
40 minutes, or until just set and golden
brown. Insert a knife into the centre of
the pudding to test if it is cooked in the
middle; the blade should come out clean.

4 Allow the pudding to cool for at least
15 minutes. Dust liberally with icing
sugar just before serving, either warm
or at room temperature.

Variations
• Try using other liqueurs – almond-
flavoured liqueur is delicious teamed
with cherries, while hazelnut, raspberry
or orange liqueurs also work well.
• Also try other fruits, such as plums,
apricots, blackberries or blueberries.

Per portion Energy 201kcal/843kJ; Protein 6.7g; Carbohydrate 23.8g, of which sugars 20.7g; Fat 8.9g, of which saturates 4.3g; Cholesterol 142mg; Calcium 89mg; Fibre 0.8g; Sodium 91mg.

Old-fashioned deep-dish apple pie

It is impossible to resist a really good home-baked apple pie. If you make your own shortcrust pastry and use eating apples bursting with flavour and loads of butter and sugar, you can't go wrong. Serve this old-fashioned dish with thick cream or nutmeg ice cream.

Serves 6

900g/2lb eating apples

75g/3oz/6 tbsp unsalted (sweet) butter

45–60ml/3–4 tbsp demerara (raw) sugar

3 cloves

2.5ml/½ tsp mixed (apple pie) spice

For the pastry

250g/9oz/2¼ cups plain (all-purpose) flour

pinch of salt

50g/2oz/¼ cup lard or white cooking fat, chilled and diced

75g/3oz/6 tbsp unsalted butter, chilled and diced

30–45ml/2–3 tbsp chilled water

a little milk, for brushing

caster (superfine) sugar, for dredging

clotted cream or ice cream, to serve

1 Preheat the oven to 200°C/400°F/Gas 6. Make the pastry first. Sift the flour and salt into a bowl. Rub in the lard or fat and butter. Stir in enough chilled water to bring the pastry together. Knead lightly, then wrap in clear film (plastic wrap) and chill for 30 minutes.

2 To make the filling, peel, core and thickly slice the apples. Melt the butter in a frying pan, add the sugar and cook for 3–4 minutes, allowing it to melt and caramelize. Add the apples and stir. Cook over a brisk heat until the apples take on a little colour, add the spices and tip out into a bowl to cool slightly.

3 Divide the pastry in two and, on a lightly floured surface, roll out into two rounds that will easily fit a deep 23cm/9in pie plate. Line the plate with one round of pastry. Spoon in the cooled filling and mound up in the centre.

4 Cover the apples with the remaining pastry, sealing and crimping the edges.

5 Make a 5cm/2in long slit through the top of the pastry to allow the steam to escape. Brush the pie with milk and dredge with caster sugar.

6 Place the pie on a baking sheet and bake in the oven for 25–35 minutes until golden and firm. Serve with dollops of thick cream or ice cream.

Per portion Energy 610kcal/2566kJ; Protein 8.1g; Carbohydrate 86.1g, of which sugars 40.2g; Fat 28.5g, of which saturates 8.8g; Cholesterol 14mg; Calcium 168mg; Fibre 8.1g; Sodium 413mg.

Boston cream pie

Actually a sponge cake filled with custard rather than cream and topped with a dark chocolate glaze, this cake is a reworking of the early American pudding cake pie.

Serves 8

225g/8oz/2 cups self-raising (self-rising) flour

15ml/1 tbsp baking powder

2.5ml/½ tsp salt

115g/4oz/½ cup butter, softened

200g/7oz/1 cup granulated (white) sugar

2 eggs

5ml/1 tsp vanilla extract

175ml/6fl oz/¾ cup milk

For the filling

250ml/8fl oz/1 cup milk

3 egg yolks

90g/3½oz/½ cup granulated (white) sugar

25g/1oz/¼ cup plain (all-purpose) flour

15g/1/2oz/1 tbsp butter

15ml/1 tbsp brandy or 5ml/1 tsp vanilla extract

For the chocolate glaze

25g/1oz cooking (unsweetened) chocolate

25g/1oz/2 tbsp butter or margarine

90g/3½oz/½ cup icing (confectioners') sugar, plus extra for dusting

2.5ml/½ tsp vanilla extract

about 15ml/1 tbsp hot water

1 Preheat the oven to 190°F/375°F/ Gas 5. Grease two 20cm/8in shallow round cake tins (pans), and line the bottoms with greased baking parchment.

2 Sift the flour with the baking powder and salt.

3 Beat the butter and granulated sugar together until light and fluffy. Add the eggs one at a time, beating well after each addition. Stir in the vanilla. Add the milk and dry ingredients alternately, mixing only enough to blend thoroughly. Do not over-beat the mixture.

4 Divide the mixture between the prepared tins and spread it out evenly. Bake until a skewer inserted in the centre comes out clean, about 25 minutes.

5 Meanwhile, make the filling. Heat the milk in a small pan to boiling point. Remove from the heat.

6 In a heatproof mixing bowl, beat the egg yolks. Gradually add the granulated sugar and continue beating until pale yellow. Beat in the flour.

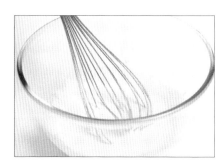

7 Pour the hot milk into the egg yolk mixture in a steady stream, beating constantly. When all the milk has been added, place the bowl over a pan of boiling water, or pour the mixture into the top of a double boiler. Heat for 30 minutes, stirring constantly, until thickened. Remove from the heat. Stir in the butter and brandy or vanilla. Chill for 2–3 hours or until set.

8 When the cake layers have cooled, use a large sharp knife to slice off the domed top to make a flat surface. Place one layer on a serving plate and spread the filling on in a thick layer. Set the other layer on top, cut side down. Smooth the edge of the filling layer so it is flush with the sides of the cake layers.

9 For the glaze, melt the chocolate with the butter or margarine in the top of a double boiler, or in a bowl over hot water. When smooth, remove from the heat and beat in the sugar to make a thick paste. Add the vanilla. Beat in a little of the hot water. If the glaze does not have a spreadable consistency, add more water, 5ml/1 tsp at a time.

10 Spread the glaze evenly over the top of the cake, using a metal spatula. Dust the top with icing sugar. Because of the custard filling, any leftover cake must be chilled in the refrigerator, and can be stored for up to 3 days.

Per portion Energy 499kcal/2099kJ; Protein 6g; Carbohydrate 77g, of which sugars 53.1g; Fat 20.3g, of which saturates 12.1g; Cholesterol 146mg; Calcium 112mg; Fibre 1g; Sodium 296mg.

Chilled berry pudding

A cross between a summer pudding and a trifle, this fragrant, light pudding makes the most of summer soft fruits and is a perfect summer dessert. Be sure to use a good loaf of bread rather than processed sliced bread, to get the best texture and flavour.

Serves 4–6

550g/1lb 4oz mixed soft fruit, such as raspberries, blackberries, blackcurrants, redcurrants

50g/2oz/4 tbsp sugar

large thick slice of bread with crusts removed, about 125g/4½oz/2 cups without crusts

300ml/½ pint/1¼ cups double (heavy) cream

45ml/3 tbsp elderflower cordial

150ml/¼ pint/⅔ cup thick natural (plain) yogurt

Cook's tip During the seasons when fresh summer fruits are not as readily available, a bag of mixed frozen fruit works just as well in this recipe.

1 Reserve a few raspberries, blackberries, blackcurrants or redcurrants for decoration, then put the remainder into a pan with the sugar and 30ml/2 tbsp water. Bring just to the boil, cover and simmer gently for 4–5 minutes, until the fruit is soft and plenty of juice has formed.

2 Cut the bread into cubes, measuring about 2.5cm/1in, and put them into one large dish or individual serving bowls or glasses.

3 Spoon the fruit mixture over the bread and leave to cool.

Variation Instead of mixing yogurt into the topping, try using the same quantity of ready-made custard – it gives a richer, sweeter result to the finished dish.

4 Whip the cream with the cordial until stiff peaks begin to form. Gently stir in the yogurt and spoon the mixture over the top of the fruit.

5 Chill until required. Just before serving, decorate the top with the reserved fruit.

Per portion Energy 382kcal/1592kJ; Protein 5.2g; Carbohydrate 29.9g, of which sugars 20.2g; Fat 27.8g, of which saturates 16.9g; Cholesterol 69mg; Calcium 124mg; Fibre 2.6g; Sodium 144mg.

Gooseberry and elderflower fool

The combination of gooseberry and elderflower is heavenly, but rhubarb and ginger or raspberries are also classic ingredients for fruit fools – you can use whatever is ripe in the kitchen garden. Serve in pretty glasses, with crisp little biscuits to add a contrast of texture.

Serves 4

500g/1¼lb gooseberries

300ml/½ pint/1¼ cups double (heavy) cream

about 115g/4oz/1 cup icing (confectioners') sugar, to taste

30ml/2 tbsp elderflower cordial

mint sprigs, to decorate

crisp biscuits (cookies), to serve

1 Place the gooseberries in a heavy pan, cover and cook over a low heat, shaking the pan occasionally, until tender. Transfer the gooseberries into a bowl, crush them with a fork or potato masher, then leave to cool completely.

2 Whip the cream until soft peaks form, then fold in half the crushed fruit. Add sugar and elderflower cordial to taste. Sweeten the remaining fruit to taste.

3 Layer the cream mixture and the crushed gooseberries in four dessert dishes or tall glasses, then cover and chill until ready to serve. Decorate the fool with mint sprigs and serve with crisp sweet biscuits.

Variations
• When in season, cook 2–3 elderflower heads with the gooseberries and omit the elderflower cordial.
• For rhubarb fool use squeezed orange juice in place of elderflower cordial.

Per portion Energy 366kcal/1521kJ; Protein 3.5g; Carbohydrate 24.2g, of which sugars 21.8g; Fat 28.4g, of which saturates 16.7g; Cholesterol 70mg; Calcium 111mg; Fibre 1.9g; Sodium 41mg.

Breads and baking

A country meal is not complete without a piece of bread, and there are few more welcoming aromas than a home-baked loaf. Doing your own baking can give great pleasure and satisfaction, and once the technique for basic dough has been mastered, there are endless variations and adaptations. This chapter also includes recipes for scones, crumpets, gingerbread and cakes – all essential country tea-time treats.

Basic yeast bread

Make this dough into any shape you like, such as braids, cottage loaves or rolls. Use strong bread flour as it has a high gluten content, making a more elastic dough that rises better.

Makes 4 loaves

25g/1oz fresh yeast

10ml/2 tsp caster (superfine) sugar

900ml/1½ pints/3¾ cups tepid water, or milk and water mixed

15ml/1 tbsp salt

1.3kg/3lb/12 cups strong white bread flour, preferably unbleached

50g/2oz/scant ¼ cup white vegetable fat (shortening) or 50ml/2fl oz/¼ cup vegetable oil

1 Cream the yeast and caster sugar together in a measuring jug (cup), add about 150ml/¼ pint/⅔ cup of the measured liquid and leave in a warm place for about 10 minutes to froth up.

2 Meanwhile, mix the salt into the flour and rub in the fat (if using oil, add it to the remaining liquid).

3 Using an electric mixer with a dough hook attachment or working by hand in a mixing bowl, add the yeast mixture and remaining liquid to the flour, and work it in to make a firm dough which leaves the bowl clean.

4 Knead well on a floured surface, or in the mixer, until the dough has become firm and elastic. Return to the bowl, cover lightly with a dish towel and leave in a warm place to rise for an hour, or until it has doubled in size. The dough will be springy and full of air. Meanwhile, oil four 450g/1lb loaf tins (pans).

5 Turn the dough out on to a floured work surface and knock back (punch down), flattening it out with your knuckles to knock the air out. Knead lightly into shape again, divide into four pieces and form into loaf shapes.

6 Place the dough in the loaf tins, pushing down well to fit into the corners, then leave to rise again for another 20–30 minutes. Meanwhile, preheat the oven to 230°C/450°F/ Gas 8.

7 When the dough has risen just above the rims of the tins, bake the loaves in the centre of the oven for 30 minutes, or until browned and shrinking a little from the sides of the tins; when turned out and rapped underneath they should sound hollow. Cool on wire racks.

Variation For Granary (whole-wheat) bread, replace the white flour with Granary flour, or half and half Granary and strong white bread flour.

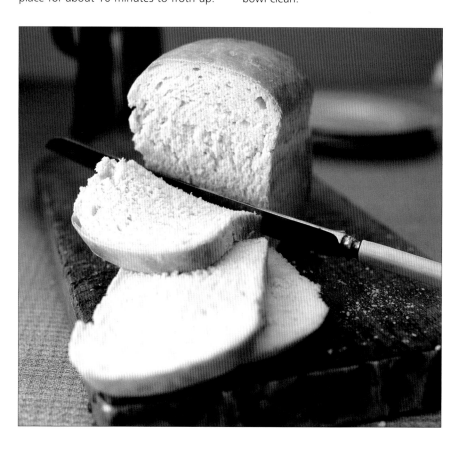

Per loaf Energy 1223kcal/5185kJ; Protein 30.7g; Carbohydrate 256.4g, of which sugars 7.5g; Fat 15.2g, of which saturates 6.3g; Cholesterol 0mg; Calcium 457mg; Fibre 10.1g; Sodium 1.48g.

Cottage loaf

Snipping both sections of the dough at 5cm/2in intervals looks attractive and also helps this classic country loaf to rise and expand in the oven while it cooks.

4 Turn out on to a lightly floured surface and knock back (punch down). Knead for 2–3 minutes, then divide the dough into two-thirds and one-third; shape each to a ball.

5 Place the balls of dough on the baking sheets. Cover with inverted bowls and leave to rise, in a warm place, for about 30 minutes. Gently flatten the top of the larger round of dough and, with a sharp knife, cut a cross in the centre, about 4cm/1½in across. Brush with a little water and place the smaller round on top.

6 Carefully press a hole through the middle of the top ball, down into the lower part, using your thumb and first two fingers. Cover with lightly oiled clear film (plastic wrap) and leave to rest in a warm place for about 10 minutes. Preheat the oven to 220°C/425°F/Gas 7 and place the bread on the lower shelf. It will finish expanding as the oven heats up. Bake for 35–40 minutes, or until golden brown. Cool on a wire rack.

Makes 1 large round loaf

675g/1½ lb/6 cups unbleached white bread flour

10ml/2 tsp salt

20g/¾ oz fresh yeast

400ml/14fl oz/1⅔ cups lukewarm water

Cook's tips
• To ensure a good-shaped cottage loaf, the dough needs to be firm enough to support the weight of the top ball.
• Alternatively, make smaller, individual rolls – bake them for 25 minutes.

1 Lightly grease two baking sheets. Sift the flour and salt together into a large bowl and make a well in the centre.

2 Mix the yeast in 150ml/¼ pint/⅔ cup of the water until dissolved. Pour into the centre of the flour with the remaining water and mix to a firm dough.

3 Knead on a lightly floured surface for 10 minutes until smooth and elastic. Place in a lightly oiled bowl, cover with lightly oiled clear film and leave to rise, in a warm place, for about 1 hour, or until doubled in bulk.

Per loaf Energy 2302kcal/9788kJ; Protein 63.5g; Carbohydrate 524.5g, of which sugars 10.1g; Fat 8.8g, of which saturates 1.4g; Cholesterol 0mg; Calcium 946mg; Fibre 20.9g; Sodium 3950mg.

Brown soda bread

Perhaps the easiest to make of all loaves, soda bread is yeast-free and so doesn't need time to rise. It is baked straightaway and is best eaten on the day it is made. It tastes delicious spread with unsalted butter and topped with a fruity jam or a slice of farmhouse cheese.

Makes 1 loaf

450g/1lb/4 cups wholemeal (whole-wheat) flour

175g/6oz/1½ cups plain (all-purpose) flour

7.5ml/1½ tsp bicarbonate of soda (baking soda)

5ml/1 tsp salt

about 450ml/¾ pint/scant 2 cups buttermilk

Variation Cream of tartar can be added to the dry ingredients to provide the acid instead of buttermilk.

1 Preheat the oven to 200°C/400°F/ Gas 6, and grease a baking sheet. Combine the dry ingredients in a mixing bowl and stir in enough buttermilk to make a fairly soft dough. Turn on to a work surface dusted with wholemeal flour and knead lightly until smooth.

2 Form the dough into a circle, about 4cm/1½in thick. Lay on the baking sheet and mark a deep cross in the top with a floured knife.

3 Bake for about 45 minutes, or until the bread is browned and sounds hollow when tapped on the base. Cool on a wire rack. If a soft crust is preferred, wrap the loaf in a clean dish towel while cooling.

Cook's tip Buttermilk can be cultured easily, using a 'buttermilk plant'. Heat 450ml/¾ pint/scant 2 cups skimmed milk to lukewarm by adding 150ml/ ¼ pint/⅔ cup boiling water, then add 25g/1oz yeast and 10ml/2 tsp sugar.
  Pour into a sterilized screw-top or preserving jar, allowing enough space for the contents to be shaken. Place on its side in a warm, dark place and shake several times a day for 4–6 days, while the buttermilk plant is forming, then remove the jar and open it carefully.
  Strain the soured milk into a jug (pitcher); the lumpy pieces of yeast left in the strainer become the buttermilk plant and can be washed and used again.
  Leftover milk can be added to the jar daily if there is room – it will thicken and sour, taking as little as 2 days in summer, 4–5 in winter.
  Remember to always wash all the old milk from the yeast and sterilize the jar.

Per loaf Energy 2262kcal/9643kJ; Protein 88.5g; Carbohydrate 465.4g, of which sugars 31.4g; Fat 18.9g, of which saturates 6.5g; Cholesterol 27mg; Calcium 1.37g; Fibre 34.2g; Sodium 2.18g.

Granary cob loaf

Bread-making can be immensely satisfying when the result is as delicious as this brown loaf. You need fresh yeast for this recipe, which has a similar texture to putty and crumbles easily when broken. Buy it in small quantities and store in the refrigerator for up to a month.

Makes 1 round loaf

450g/1lb/4 cups Granary (whole-wheat) or malthouse flour

12.5ml/2½ tsp salt

15g/½oz fresh yeast

wheat flakes or cracked wheat, for sprinkling

1 Lightly flour a baking sheet. Mix the flour and 10ml/2 tsp of the salt together in a large bowl and make a well in the centre. Place in a very low oven for 5 minutes to warm.

2 Measure 300ml/½ pint/1¼ cups lukewarm water. Mix the yeast with a little of the water, then blend in the rest. Pour the yeast mixture into the centre of the flour and mix to a dough.

3 Turn out on to a lightly floured surface and knead for about 10 minutes, until smooth and elastic. Place in a lightly oiled bowl, cover with lightly oiled clear film (plastic wrap) and leave to rise in a warm place for 1¼ hours, or until doubled in bulk.

4 Turn the dough out on to a floured surface. Knead for 2–3 minutes, then roll into a ball. Place on the baking sheet. Cover with a bowl and leave to rise in a warm place for 30–45 minutes.

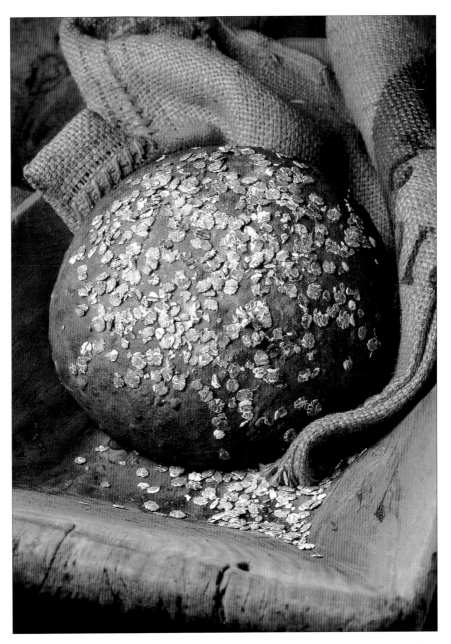

5 Preheat the oven to 230°C/450°F/ Gas 8 towards the end of the rising time. Mix 30ml/2 tbsp water with the remaining salt and brush evenly over the bread. Sprinkle the loaf with wheat flakes, cracked wheat or a handful of rolled oats.

6 Bake the bread for 15 minutes, then reduce the oven temperature to 200°C/400°F/Gas 6 and bake for a further 20 minutes, or until the loaf is firm to the touch and sounds hollow when tapped on the base. Cool on a wire rack.

Per loaf Energy 1395kcal/5931kJ; Protein 57.1g; Carbohydrate 287.6g, of which sugars 9.4g; Fat 9.9g, of which saturates 1.4g; Cholesterol 0mg; Calcium 172mg; Fibre 40.5g; Sodium 4926mg.

Bara brith fruited teabread

The name for this traditional Welsh loaf means 'speckled bread'. For a hint of citrus, add grated lemon or orange rind to the batter before baking. Spread with butter and honey.

Makes 1 large loaf

225g/8oz/1⅓ cups mixed dried fruit and chopped mixed (candied) peel

225ml/8fl oz/1 cup hot strong tea, strained

225g/8oz/2 cups self-raising (self-rising) flour

5ml/1 tsp mixed (apple pie) spice

25g/1oz/2 tbsp butter

100g/3½oz/8 tbsp soft brown sugar

1 egg, lightly beaten

Cook's tip The flavour of the loaf can be varied subtly by using a variety of teas – try the distinctive perfume of Earl Grey.

1 Put the fruit into a heatproof bowl and pour the hot tea over it. Cover and leave to stand at room temperature for several hours or overnight.

2 Preheat the oven to 180°C/350°F/ Gas 4. Grease a 900g/2lb loaf tin (pan) and line it with baking parchment.

3 Sift the flour and the mixed spice into a large mixing bowl. Add the butter and, with your fingertips, rub it into the flour until the mixture starts to resemble fine breadcrumbs.

4 Stir the soft brown sugar into the flour and spice mixture, then add the dried fruit and its liquid along with the beaten egg. Stir well with a wooden spoon to make a mixture with a soft consistency.

5 Transfer the mixture to the prepared loaf tin and level the surface. Put into the hot oven and cook for about 1 hour or until a skewer inserted in the centre comes out clean. Turn out on a wire rack and leave to cool completely.

Per loaf Energy 2024kcal/8588kJ; Protein 33.2g; Carbohydrate 432.7g, of which sugars 261.3g; Fat 29.9g, of which saturates 15g; Cholesterol 244mg; Calcium 565mg; Fibre 11.9g; Sodium 342mg.

Walnut and caramelized onion scones

These savoury scones are delicious served warm with butter, artisan cheese and fruit chutney. They can be made as small scones for a party, topped with cheese or cold meat.

Makes 10–12

90g/3½oz/7 tbsp butter or non-hydrogenated margarine

15ml/1 tbsp olive oil

1 Spanish (Bermuda) onion, chopped

5ml/1 tsp cumin seeds, lightly crushed

200g/7oz/1¾ cups self-raising (self-rising) flour

5ml/1 tsp baking powder

25g/1oz/¼ cup fine oatmeal

5ml/1 tsp light unrefined muscovado (brown) sugar

90g/3½oz/scant 1 cup chopped walnuts

5ml/1 tsp chopped fresh thyme

120–150ml/4–5fl oz/½–⅔ cup buttermilk

a little milk or soya milk

sea salt and ground black pepper

1 Melt 15g/½oz/1 tbsp of the butter with the oil in a small pan and cook the onion gently, covered, for 10–12 minutes. Uncover, then continue to cook gently until it begins to brown.

2 Add half the cumin seeds and increase the heat slightly. Continue to cook, stirring occasionally, until the onion begins to caramelize. Cool. Preheat the oven to 200°C/400°F/Gas 6.

3 Sift the flour and baking powder into a large bowl and add the oatmeal, sugar, 2.5ml/½ tsp salt and black pepper. Add the remaining butter or margarine and rub in until the mixture resembles fine breadcrumbs.

4 Add the cooked onion and cumin mixture, chopped walnuts and chopped fresh thyme, then bind to make a soft, but not sticky, dough with the buttermilk.

5 Roll or pat out the mixture to an even thickness of just over 1cm/½in. Stamp out 10–12 scones using a 5–6cm/ 2–2½in plain round cutter.

6 Place the scones on a floured baking tray, glaze with the milk or soya milk and scatter with a little salt and the remaining cumin seeds. Bake the scones for 12–15 minutes until well-risen and golden brown. Allow to cool for a few minutes on a wire rack and serve warm spread with butter, non-hydrogenated margarine or goat's cheese.

Per portion Energy 131kcal/543kJ; Protein 1.8g; Carbohydrate 3g, of which sugars 1.3g; Fat 12.6g, of which saturates 4.6g; Cholesterol 17mg; Calcium 23mg; Fibre 0.5g; Sodium 51mg.

Scones with jam and cream

For many people, English afternoon tea without a plate of scones would be unthinkable. Quick and easy to make, these are best served fresh and warm from the oven. Top with cream and jam or soft fruits in the summer, and bottled or preserved fruits in the winter.

Makes about 12

450g/1lb/4 cups self-raising (self-rising) flour, or 450g/1lb/ 4 cups plain (all-purpose) flour and 10ml/2 tsp baking powder

5ml/1 tsp salt

55g/2oz/¼ cup butter, chilled and cut into small cubes

15ml/1 tbsp lemon juice

about 400ml/14fl oz/1⅔ cups milk, plus extra to glaze

butter, jam and cream, to serve

1 Preheat the oven to 230°C/450°F/ Gas 8. Sift the flour, baking powder (if using) and salt into a mixing bowl, and stir to mix through. Add the butter and rub it lightly into the flour with your fingertips until the mixture resembles fine, even-textured breadcrumbs.

2 Whisk the lemon juice into the milk and leave for about 1 minute to thicken slightly, then pour into the flour mixture and mix quickly to make a soft but pliable dough. The softer the mixture, the lighter the resulting scones will be, but if it is too sticky they will spread during baking and lose their shape.

3 Knead the dough briefly, then roll it out on a lightly floured surface to a thickness of at least 2.5cm/1in. Using a 5cm/2in biscuit (cookie) cutter, and dipping it into flour each time, stamp out 12 rounds. Place the dough rounds on a well-floured baking sheet. Re-roll the trimmings and cut out more scones.

4 Brush the tops with a little milk, then put into the hot oven and cook for about 20 minutes, or until risen.

5 Remove from the oven and wrap the scones in a clean dish towel to keep them warm and soft until ready to eat. Eat the scones with butter, plenty of jam and a generous dollop of clotted or whipped double (heavy) cream.

Variation To make savoury cheese scones, add 115g/4oz/1 cup of grated cheese, such as mature (sharp) Cheddar, to the dough and knead it in thoroughly before rolling out and cutting into shapes.

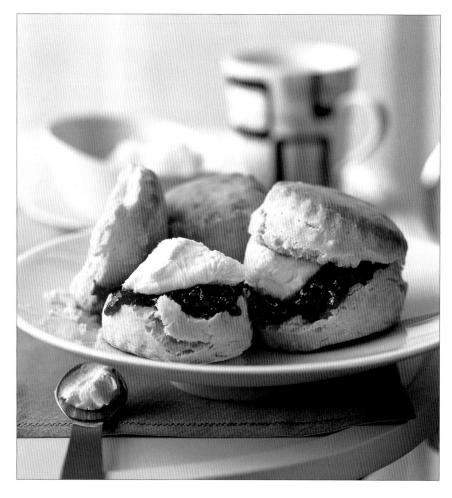

Per portion Energy 177kcal/749kJ; Protein 4.7g; Carbohydrate 30.7g, of which sugars 2.2g; Fat 4.8g, of which saturates 2.8g; Cholesterol 12mg; Calcium 93mg; Fibre 1.2g; Sodium 43mg.

Tea-time crumpets

Toasting English crumpets on an open fire is a country tradition. These are made with a yeast batter and cooked in metal rings on a griddle. They are equally tasty with either savoury or sweet toppings – try golden syrup, honey or preserves, or sliced ham or cheese.

Makes about 10

225g/8oz/2 cups plain (all-purpose) flour

2.5ml/½ tsp salt

2.5ml/½ tsp bicarbonate of soda (baking soda)

5ml/1 tsp fast-action yeast granules

150ml/¼ pint/⅔ cup milk

oil, for greasing

1 Sift the flour, salt and bicarbonate of soda into a bowl and stir in the yeast. Make a well in the centre. Heat the milk with 200ml/7fl oz/scant 1 cup water until lukewarm and tip into the well.

2 Mix well with a whisk or wooden spoon, beating vigorously to make a thick smooth batter. Cover and leave in a warm place for about 1 hour until the mixture has a spongy texture. Re-whisk the batter before cooking.

3 Heat a griddle or heavy frying pan. Lightly oil the hot surface and the inside of three or four metal rings, each measuring about 8cm/3½in in diameter. Place the oiled rings on the hot surface and leave for 1–2 minutes until hot.

4 Spoon the batter into the rings to a depth of about 1cm/½in. Cook over a medium-high heat for about 6 minutes until the top surface is set and bubbles have burst open to make holes.

5 When set, carefully lift off the metal rings and flip the crumpets over, cooking the second side for just 1 minute until lightly browned.

6 Lift off and leave to cool completely on a wire rack. Repeat with the remaining crumpet mixture. Just before serving, toast the crumpets on both sides and butter generously.

Per portion Energy 93kcal/393kJ; Protein 3g; Carbohydrate 16.5g, of which sugars 1g; Fat 2.1g, of which saturates 1g; Cholesterol 21mg; Calcium 48mg; Fibre 0.6g; Sodium 21mg.

Dark and sticky gingerbread

This is a really special gingerbread. The secret of its dark, rich stickiness lies in the huge amount of treacle used. It is very tactile and literally sticks to the roof of your mouth when you eat it. Slice and serve with butter or cream cheese, or spread with vanilla butter icing.

Makes an 18cm/7in square cake

225g/8oz/2 cups plain
(all-purpose) flour

10ml/2 tsp ground ginger

5ml/1 tsp mixed (apple pie) spice

a pinch of salt

2 pieces stem (preserved) ginger,
drained and chopped

115g/4oz/½ cup butter, softened

115g/4oz/¾ cup dark muscovado
(molasses) sugar, sifted

275g/10oz/scant 1 cup black treacle
(molasses), at room temperature

2 eggs, beaten

2.5ml/½ tsp bicarbonate of soda
(baking soda)

30ml/2 tbsp milk, warmed

butter or cream cheese, to serve

1 Preheat the oven to 160°C/325°F/ Gas 3. Grease and line the base of an 18cm/7in square cake tin (pan) that measures about 7.5cm/3in deep.

2 Sift the flour, ground ginger, mixed spice and salt into a bowl. Add the ginger and toss it in the flour to coat.

3 Cream the butter and sugar together until fluffy, then gradually stir in the treacle. Gradually beat in the eggs, then the flour mixture.

4 Dissolve the bicarbonate of soda in the milk and gradually beat this into the mixture. Pour the mixture into the prepared tin and bake for 45 minutes.

5 Reduce the oven temperature to 150°C/300°F/Gas 2 and bake for a further 30 minutes. The gingerbread should look very dark and slightly risen. Remove the tray from the oven and check the cake is cooked by inserting a metal skewer into the middle. If it comes out clean, the cake is done. Don't worry if the gingerbread sinks slightly in the middle – it always does.

6 Cool the gingerbread for 5 minutes in the tin, then turn out and cool on a wire rack. At this stage, the gingerbread will be dark, but not sticky at all. Keep it for 2–3 days in an airtight container and the outside will become sticky and moist. Slice when ready, then spread with butter or cream cheese.

Per cake Energy 2274kcal/9594kJ; Protein 36.7g; Carbohydrate 399g, of which sugars 252.9g; Fat 70g, of which saturates 28.3g; Cholesterol 11mg; Calcium 589mg; Fibre 21.1g; Sodium 928mg.

Old-fashioned treacle cake

Quick to make and very moreish, this fruit-studded, crumbly cake hails from Wales and would have originally been baked on a tin plate. The black treacle gives the cake both a rich colour and deep flavour, and a generous wedge would be a welcome treat at any lunch.

Makes a 20cm/8in cake

250g/9oz/2 cups self-raising (self-rising) flour

2.5ml/½ tsp mixed (apple pie) spice

75g/3oz/6 tbsp butter, cut into cubes

35g/1oz/2 tbsp caster (superfine) sugar

150g/5oz/1 cup mixed dried fruit

1 egg

15ml/1 tbsp black treacle (molasses)

100ml/3½fl oz/scant ½ cup milk

3 Beat the egg and, with a small whisk or a fork, stir in the treacle and then the milk. Stir the liquid into the flour to make a fairly stiff but moist consistency, adding a little extra milk if necessary.

4 Transfer the cake mixture to the prepared dish or tin with a spoon and level out the surface.

5 Bake the cake in the hot oven and cook for about 1 hour until it has risen, is firm to the touch and fully cooked through. To check if the cake is cooked, insert a small skewer in the centre – it should come out free of sticky mixture.

6 Leave the cooked treacle cake to cool completely. Serve it straight from the dish, cut into wedges.

1 Preheat the oven to 180°C/350°F/ Gas 5. Butter a shallow 20–23cm/ 8–9in ovenproof flan dish or baking tin (pan).

2 Sift the flour and spice into a large mixing bowl. Add the butter and, with your fingertips, rub it into the flour until the mixture resembles fine crumbs. Alternatively, you could do this in a food processor. Stir in the sugar and mixed dried fruit.

Variation Try varying the fruit in this recipe. Experiment with chopped ready-to-eat dried apricots and stem ginger, or a packet of luxury dried fruit. Chopped dates or figs work well too, and make the cake more substantial.

Per cake Energy 2089kcal/8805kJ; Protein 37.4g; Carbohydrate 343g, of which sugars 152.4g; Fat 72.8g, of which saturates 42.2g; Cholesterol 356mg; Calcium 720mg; Fibre 11.1g; Sodium 676mg.

Victoria sponge

This light cake was named in honour of England's Queen Victoria, and is a favourite at baking competitions. It is based on equal quantities of fat, sugar, eggs and flour. Fill with jam or preserves of your choice, or soft summer fruits such as strawberries or raspberries.

Serves 6–8

3 large eggs

few drops of vanilla extract

175g/6oz/¾ cup soft butter

175g/6oz/¾ cup caster (superfine) sugar

175g/6oz/1½ cups self-raising (self-rising) flour

about 60ml/4 tbsp jam

icing (confectioners') sugar, to dust

1 Preheat the oven to 180°C/350°F/ Gas 4. Butter two 20cm/8in sandwich tins (layer pans) and line the bases of each with baking parchment.

2 Lightly beat the eggs with the vanilla extract. In a large mixing bowl, whisk the butter with the sugar until the mixture is pale, light and fluffy.

3 Gradually add the eggs, beating well after each addition. Sift the flour over the top and, using a metal spoon, fold in lightly until the mixture is smooth.

4 Divide the mixture between the prepared tins. Cook for 20 minutes until golden and firm to the touch.

5 Leave the cakes to cool in the tins for a few minutes then carefully turn out on to a wire rack. Remove the paper and leave to cool completely.

6 When the cakes are cold, sandwich the two halves together with plenty of jam. Finally, sift a little icing sugar over the top to cover the surface of the cake.

Variations

• Instead of vanilla extract, beat a little finely grated lemon rind into the butter and sugar mixture in step 2. Sandwich the cakes together with lemon curd.
• For a cream cake, sandwich with a thin layer of strawberry jam and a thick layer of whipped cream, topped with sliced fresh strawberries. Decorate the top of the cake with whipped cream and extra strawberries.

Per portion Energy 368kcal/1543kJ; Protein 4.6g; Carbohydrate 44.7g, of which sugars 28.5g; Fat 20.3g, of which saturates 12g; Cholesterol 118mg; Calcium 104mg; Fibre 0.7g; Sodium 241mg.

Rich chocolate cake with chocolate icing

Chocolate cake is a staple of every self-respecting country tea table. A luxurious afternoon treat, this impressive cake with chocolate buttercream would look even more tempting topped with toasted half walnuts, pecans or hazelnuts. Serve with tea or coffee.

Serves 10–12

225g/8oz/2 cups plain (all-purpose) flour

5ml/1 tsp bicarbonate of soda (baking soda)

50g/2oz/½ cup (unsweetened) cocoa powder

125g/4½oz/9 tbsp soft butter

250g/9oz/1¼ cups caster (superfine) sugar

3 eggs, beaten

250ml/8fl oz/1 cup buttermilk

For the chocolate buttercream

175g/6oz/1½ cups icing (confectioners') sugar

115g/4oz/½ cup soft unsalted (sweet) butter

few drops of vanilla extract

50g/2oz dark (bittersweet) chocolate

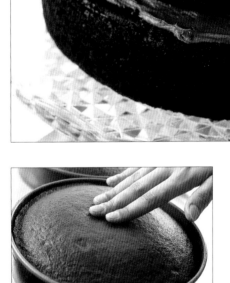

5 Beat in half the sifted icing sugar until smooth and light. Gradually beat in the remaining sugar and the vanilla extract. Break the chocolate into squares. Melt in a bowl over a pan of hot water or in a microwave oven on low.

1 Butter two 20cm/8in sandwich tins (layer pans) and line the bases with baking parchment. Preheat the oven to 180°C/350°F/Gas 4. Sift the flour with the bicarbonate of soda and cocoa and stir together.

2 Beat the butter and sugar until light and fluffy. Gradually beat in the eggs. Add the flour and buttermilk; mix well.

3 Spoon into the prepared tins. Place into the hot oven and cook for 30–35 minutes until firm to the touch. Turn out of the tins, peel off the paper and leave on a wire rack to cool completely.

4 To make the chocolate buttercream, sift the icing sugar into a bowl. In a separate bowl, beat the butter until very soft and creamy.

6 Mix the melted chocolate into the buttercream. Use half to sandwich the cakes together, and the rest on the top.

Per portion Energy 430kcal/1790kJ; Protein 7.8g; Carbohydrate 29.5g, of which sugars 28.8g; Fat 32.1g, of which saturates 13.6g; Cholesterol 96mg; Calcium 92mg; Fibre 1.9g; Sodium 125mg.

Preserves and relishes

As well as preserving the taste of summer fruits and vegetables, it is immensely satisfying to make your own jams, jellies and relishes. Country-style home-made ones always taste better than store-bought varieties, and also make lovely gifts. Spicy and fruity relishes enliven the simplest of rustic dishes, and stirring a bubbling pot of preserves is a highly pleasurable pastime – both easy and rewarding.

Blackcurrant jam

Dark, jewelled blackcurrants look and taste fabulous in this classic fruity jam. Serve on hot buttered toast, crumpets or croissants, or use as a filling for cakes.

Makes about 1.3kg/3lb

1.3kg/3lb/12 cups blackcurrants

grated rind and juice of 1 orange

475ml/16fl oz/2 cups water

1.3kg/3lb/6½ cups granulated (white) sugar, warmed

30ml/2 tbsp cassis (optional)

1 Place the blackcurrants, orange rind and juice and water in a large heavy pan. Bring to the boil, reduce the heat and simmer for 30 minutes.

2 Add the warmed sugar to the pan and stir over a low heat until the sugar has dissolved.

3 Bring the mixture to the boil and cook for about 8 minutes, or until the jam reaches setting point (105°C/220°F).

4 Remove the pan from the heat and skim off any scum from the surface using a slotted spoon.

5 Leave to cool for 5 minutes, then stir in the cassis, if using.

6 Pour the jam into warmed sterilized jars and seal. Leave the jars to cool completely, then label and store in a cool, dark place. The jam will keep for up to 6 months.

Per portion Energy 5504kcal/23,503kJ; Protein 18.4g; Carbohydrate 1448.7g, of which sugars 1448.7g; Fat 0.1g, of which saturates 0g; Cholesterol 0mg; Calcium 1474mg; Fibre 46.9g; Sodium 122mg.

Spiced cider jelly

This wonderfully spicy jelly goes well with cheese and crackers, or can simply be spread on to warm toast. It is also good spooned into rice pudding or added to apple pie filling.

Makes about 1.3kg/3lb

900g/2lb tart cooking apples, washed and coarsely chopped, with skins and cores intact

900ml/1¼ pints/3¾ cups sweet cider

juice and pips (seeds) of 2 oranges

1 cinnamon stick

6 whole cloves

150ml/½ pint/⅔ cup water

about 900g/2lb/4½ cups preserving or granulated (white) sugar, warmed

1 Put the apples, cider, juice and pips, cinnamon, cloves and water in a large pan. Bring to the boil, cover and simmer for about 1 hour.

2 Leave to cool slightly, then pour the fruit into a scalded jelly bag suspended over a non-metallic bowl and leave to drain overnight.

3 Measure the strained juice into a preserving pan. Add 450g/1lb/ 2¼ cups warmed sugar for every 600ml/1 pint/2½ cups juice.

4 Heat, stirring, over a low heat until the sugar has dissolved. Increase the heat and boil, without stirring, for 10 minutes, or until the jelly reaches setting point (105°C/220°F).

5 Remove from the heat and skim off any scum. Ladle into warmed sterilized jars. Leave to cool, then cover, seal and label the jars. Store in a dark cupboard for up to 6 months.

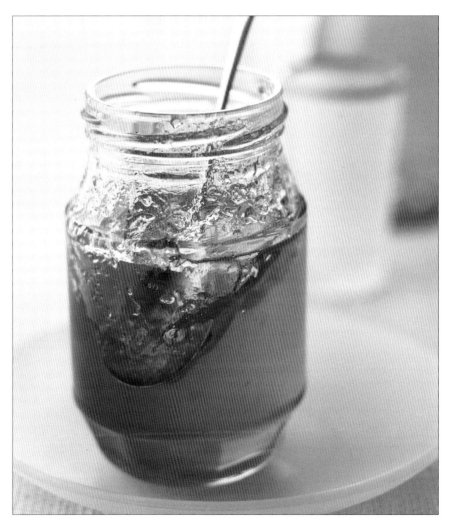

Per portion Energy 3975kcal/16,950kJ; Protein 5.4g; Carbohydrate 990.6g, of which sugars 990.6g; Fat 0.3g, of which saturates 0g; Cholesterol 0mg; Calcium 561mg; Fibre 4.8g; Sodium 123mg.

Plum and cherry relish

This simple sweet-and-sour fruit relish complements rich poultry, game or meat, such as roast duck or grilled duck breasts. You can sieve a few spoonfuls into a sauce or gravy to give fruity zest and flavour, as well as adding an appetizing splash of bright red colour.

1 Halve and pit the plums, then roughly chop the flesh. Pit all the cherries and cut them in half.

2 Cook the shallots gently in the oil for 5 minutes, or until soft. Add the fruit, sherry, vinegars, bay leaf and sugar.

3 Slowly bring the mixture to the boil, stirring until the sugar has dissolved completely. Increase the heat and cook briskly for about 15 minutes, or until the relish is very thick and the fruit tender.

Makes about 350g/12oz

350g/12oz dark-skinned red plums

350g/12oz/2 cups cherries

2 shallots, finely chopped

15ml/1 tbsp olive oil

30ml/2 tbsp dry sherry

60ml/4 tbsp red wine vinegar

15ml/1 tbsp balsamic vinegar

1 bay leaf

90g/3½oz/scant ½ cup demerara (raw) sugar

4 Remove the bay leaf and spoon the relish into warmed sterilized jars. Cover and seal. Store the relish in the refrigerator and use within 3 months.

Cook's tip Use a large preserving pan in which the mixture comes only half-way up the side. Always use just-ripe or slightly under-ripe fruits, as the pectin levels reduce when the fruit ripens. Pectin is essential to achieve a good set.

Per portion Energy 804kcal/3407kJ; Protein 6.5g; Carbohydrate 170.3g, of which sugars 168.9g; Fat 11.8g, of which saturates 1.6g; Cholesterol 0mg; Calcium 156mg; Fibre 9.6g; Sodium 21mg.

Green tomato chutney

This is a classic chutney for using the last tomatoes of summer that just never seem to ripen. Apples and onions contribute essential flavour, which is enhanced by the addition of spice. This zesty chutney is good in sandwiches, for barbecues and with burgers.

Makes about 2.5kg/5½lb

1.8kg/4lb green tomatoes, chopped

450g/1lb cooking apples, peeled, cored and chopped

450g/1lb onions, chopped

2 large garlic cloves, crushed

15ml/1 tbsp salt

45ml/3 tbsp pickling spice

600ml/1 pint/2½ cups cider vinegar

450g/1lb/2¼ cups granulated (white) sugar

1 Place the tomatoes, apples, onions and garlic in a large pan and add the salt.

2 Tie the pickling spice in a piece of muslin (cheesecloth) and add to the ingredients in the pan.

3 Add half the vinegar to the pan and bring to the boil. Reduce the heat, then simmer for 1 hour, or until the chutney is reduced and thick, stirring frequently.

4 Put the sugar and remaining vinegar in a pan and heat gently until the sugar has dissolved, then add to the chutney. Simmer for 1½ hours until thick, stirring the mixture occasionally.

5 Remove the muslin bag from the chutney, then spoon the hot chutney into warmed sterilized jars. Cover and seal immediately. Allow the chutney to mature for at least 1 month before using.

Per portion Energy 2398kcal/10,233kJ; Protein 21.6g; Carbohydrate 601.7g, of which sugars 591.3g; Fat 6.8g, of which saturates 1.8g; Cholesterol 0mg; Calcium 495mg; Fibre 31.5g; Sodium 2177mg.

Sweet piccalilli

Undoubtedly one of the most popular relishes, piccalilli can be eaten with grilled sausages, ham, chops or cold meats, or a strong, well-flavoured cheese such as Cheddar. It should contain a good selection of fresh, crunchy vegetables in a smooth mustard sauce.

Makes about 1.8kg/4lb

1 large cauliflower

450g/1lb pickling (pearl) onions

900g/2lb mixed vegetables, such as marrow (large zucchini), cucumber, French (green) beans

225g/8oz/1 cup salt

2.4 litres/4 pints/10 cups cold water

200g/7oz/1 cup granulated (white) sugar

2 garlic cloves, peeled and crushed

10ml/2 tsp mustard powder

5ml/1 tsp ground ginger

1 litre/1^3⁄4 pints/4 cups distilled (white) vinegar

25g/1oz/¼ cup plain (all-purpose) flour

15ml/1 tbsp turmeric

Cook's tip Traditional preserving pans are copper, but if you don't have a preserving pan, any stainless steel, shallow and wide-topped pan will be suitable – this will aid evaporation and give a good result.

1 Prepare the vegetables. Divide the cauliflower into small florets; peel and quarter the pickling onions; seed and finely dice the marrow and cucumber; top and tail the French beans, then cut them into 2.5cm/1in lengths.

2 Layer the vegetables in a large glass or stainless steel bowl, generously sprinkling each layer with salt. Pour over the water, cover the bowl with clear film (plastic wrap) and leave to soak for about 24 hours.

3 Drain the soaked vegetables and discard the brine. Rinse well in several changes of cold water to remove as much salt as possible, then drain them thoroughly.

4 Put the sugar, garlic, mustard, ginger and 900ml/1½ pints/3¾ cups of the vinegar in a preserving pan. Heat gently, stirring occasionally, until the sugar has dissolved.

5 Add the vegetables to the pan, bring to the boil, reduce the heat and simmer for 10–15 minutes, or until they are almost tender.

6 Mix the flour and turmeric with the remaining vinegar and stir into the vegetables. Bring to the boil, stirring, and simmer for 5 minutes, until the piccalilli is thick.

7 Spoon the piccalilli into warmed sterilized jars, cover and seal. Store in a cool, dark place for at least 2 weeks. Use within 1 year.

Per portion Energy 1358kcal/5757kJ; Protein 34.1g; Carbohydrate 300.8g, of which sugars 266g; Fat 12g, of which saturates 1.2g; Cholesterol 0mg; Calcium 555mg; Fibre 20.6g; Sodium 4011mg.

Moutarde aux fines herbes

This fragrant, hot mustard may be used either as a delicious condiment or for coating meats such as chicken and pork, or oily fish such as mackerel, before cooking. It is also fabulous when smeared thinly on cheese on toast, for an added bite.

Makes about 300ml/½ pint/1¼ cups

75g/3oz/scant ½ cup white mustard seeds

50g/2oz/¼ cup soft light brown sugar

5ml/1 tsp salt

5ml/1 tsp whole peppercorns

2.5ml/½ tsp ground turmeric

200ml/7fl oz/scant 1 cup distilled malt vinegar

60ml/4 tbsp chopped fresh mixed herbs, such as parsley, sage, thyme and rosemary

1 Put the mustard seeds, sugar, salt, whole peppercorns and ground turmeric into a food processor or blender and process for about 1 minute, or until the peppercorns are coarsely chopped.

2 Gradually add the vinegar to the mustard mixture, 15ml/1 tbsp at a time, processing well between each addition, then continue processing until a coarse paste forms.

3 Add the chopped fresh herbs to the mustard and mix well, then leave to stand for 10–15 minutes until the mustard thickens slightly.

4 Spoon the mustard into a 300ml/ ½ pint/1¼ cup sterilized jar. Cover the surface of the mustard with a baking parchment disc, then seal with a screw-top lid or a cork, and label. Store in a cool, dark place for up to 3 months.

Per portion Energy 553kcal/2324kJ; Protein 23.4g; Carbohydrate 69.1g, of which sugars 53.4g; Fat 34.5g, of which saturates 1.1g; Cholesterol 3mg; Calcium 374mg; Fibre 2.5g; Sodium 23mg.

Honey mustard

Delicious home-made mustards mature to make the most aromatic of condiments. This honey mustard is richly flavoured and is wonderful served with meats and cheeses, or stirred into sauces and salad dressings to give an extra peppery bite. The addition of honey gives a sweet counterbalance to the hot mustard seeds.

Makes about 500g/1¼lb

225g/8oz/1 cup mustard seeds

15ml/1 tbsp ground cinnamon

2.5ml/½ tsp ground ginger

300ml/½ pint/1½ cups white wine vinegar

90ml/6 tbsp dark clear honey

Cook's tip Use well-flavoured clear honey for this recipe. Set (crystallized) honey does not have the right consistency and will not work well.

1 Put the mustard seeds in a bowl with the cinnamon and ginger, and pour over the white wine vinegar. Stir well to mix, then cover and leave to soak overnight in a cool place.

2 The next day, put the mustard mixture in a mortar and pound with a pestle, adding the honey very gradually.

3 Continue pounding and mixing until the mustard resembles a stiff paste. If the mixture becomes too stiff, add a little extra vinegar to achieve the desired consistency.

4 Spoon the mustard into four warmed sterilized jars. Seal and label the jars, then store in a cool, dark place or in the refrigerator. Keep refrigerated after opening, and use within 4 weeks.

Per portion Energy 1276kcal/5345kJ; Protein 65.4g; Carbohydrate 115.3g, of which sugars 68.8g; Fat 101.5g, of which saturates 3.4g; Cholesterol 9mg; Calcium 747mg; Fibre 0g; Sodium 21mg.

Index

Picture acknowledgements

t=top, b=bottom, l=left, r=right
iStockphoto: 11t, 27b, 28t, 29tl, 29tr, 32bl.